Forging a Kaizen Culture

Utilizing Muda-tori to Eliminate Waste and Uncover Lean Leadership

T0384923

Forging a Kaizen Culture

Utilizing Muda-tori to Eliminate Waste and Uncover Lean Leadership

Hitoshi Yamada

Originally published as *Shop Floor Kaikaku: Muda-tori is the Unbeatable Management System*, copyright 2009 Hitoshi Yamada.

English translation © 2011 by Enna Products Corporation.

For Academic and Quantity Discounts Contact Enna
Toll Free: 866-249-7348 or email info@enna.com

Address all comments and inquiries to:
Enna Products Corporation
1602 Carolina St.
Unit B3
Bellingham, WA 98229
Telephone: (360) 306-5369
Fax: (905) 481-0756
E-mail: info@enna.com

Distributed by Productivity Press, an imprint of CRC Press
711 Third Avenue, New York, NY 10017
2 Park Square, Milton Park, Abingdon, Oxon OX14 4RN
www.productivitypress.com

CRC Press is an imprint of the Taylor & Francis Group, an informa business

Printed in the United States of America

Library of Congress Control Number: 2011940509
Library of Congress Cataloging-in-Publication Data
Yamada, Hitoshi
Forging a Kaizen Culture
Includes index.
ISBN 978-1-926537-40-5
1. Operations Management (BUS049000)
2. Organizational Development (BUS103000)
3. Business Development (BUS092000)
4. Industries/Manufacturing (BUS070050)

Written by Hitoshi Yamada

Cover by Antonio Mendez
Editor Collin McLoughlin
Associate Editor Shawna Gilleland

Table of Contents

CHAPTER 2

ESCAPING FROM MASS PRODUCTION 31

Chapter 3

Management that Makes Muda-tori Successful   67

Chapter 4

Why is Muda Invisible to You?   93

CHAPTER 5

List of Figures

List of Photos

Acknowledgements

This book would not be possible were it not for the hard work of the following people: Ms. Yoko Sato, for her work in translation from the original Japanese text; Shawna Gilleland, for her careful editing and layout design; and Antonio Mendez for his diligent reproduction of the illustrations in English and creation of the cover design. Finally, I would like to thank Mr. Jun Nakamuro for discovering this gem of a book and bringing it to our attention, so that we are able to share Mr. Yamada's insights with the world.

Collin McLoughlin
Publisher

Mr. Yamada and his Apprentice, Mr. Toshihiko Miura

"Sensei Yamada taught all of us, by his examples on the shop floor, that only Muda-tori can fully develop each worker's leadership potential. This leads the company to experience exponential success."

- Toshihiko Miura

Foreword

The key to excellence for any organization is its management system and how employees are empowered to fulfill organizational objectives. Are employees given the tools to allow them to explore better methods to achieve these objectives? Has management provided the systemized structure to link organizational goals to individual accomplishments? If not, management needs to apply this kind of thinking to become valuable in their role as employees – to providing this necessary link.

Their role is to instill a self-management leadership structure within the organization so that management can allow employees to make decisions, knowing that they will come up with results utilizing the correct principles, thinking, and methodology. Through this structure they will then create ideas that are more innovative than management thought possible. This is the concept of creating a standard that can be built upon, time and time again. A standard system will spread throughout the organization, transcending hierarchy and empowering employees to develop and modify new standards to build upon.

It is important to empower workers to think beyond just themselves within the organization and realize that they have the freedom to remove wastes from their entire workplace. With management firmly creating a system where only the right choice can be made through the use of visual management techniques (management boards everyone can see & read, signs, andon, etc.), standards, Kaizen systems, and more, trust and appreciation is shown to the workers, who then feel free enough to experiment and explore their independence.

This independence, when nurtured and supported by management, will bring employees face to face with operational challenges. They will employ their knowledge, learn new skills, and cooperate with each other to overcome these challenges and a new set of standards and an open-communication culture will develop. Employees who are faced daily with challenges to overcome and a work environment that trusts them to make positive changes will soon work together proactively to innovate and eliminate wasteful activities from their workplace.

This removal of waste and engagement in their

workplace is the main principle behind Muda-tori. Muda-tori is a management system which focuses on the complete elimination of waste to re-discover the livelihood of workers and bring a sense of joy and pride back into the workforce. Waste in this context, however, is far more than the typical 7 Wastes talked about in Lean Manufacturing. Instead, the focus is on all waste, in both the workplace and in everyday life in general. Anywhere waste can be found it can be eliminated to improve the quality of a process, flow, product, service, or experience.

The biggest waste in the manufacturing industry has stemmed from the Mass Production System, resulting in the division of labor. This system essentially takes away all individuality and demands workers only master a single skill to complete only a part of a finished product or service. The only improvement a worker is allowed to do is increase the speed at which they utilize their single skill; for instance, to attempt to keep up with a conveyor line to try and reduce WIP accumulation. There is nothing more de-motivating than simply performing the same task, day in and day out, repeatedly.

Once an employee's motivation to use their intellect is taken away there can be no further progress toward a more ideal state of work. If, however, an organization focuses on creating flexible, multi-skilled workers, there is no limit to the amount of progress that can be made. It was once a normal occurrence for a worker to take pride in their job, strive to work faster, with better quality, and enjoy the support of the management team in creating a new standard of work. This mentality can often still be found in smaller organizations, but larger companies struggle with this concept.

Muda-tori is a management system which strives to revive peoples' livelihood and help each worker find joy in his/her work. It has been found, over the last 30 years, that workplace fulfillment translates to motivation and fulfillment in the rest of a person's life, and a workplace free of waste, or Muda, is a satisfying workplace.

Collin McLoughlin
President, Enna

Yamada's Lean Lesson No. 1

"Eyes to see Muda;
Courage to eliminate Muda;
Wisdom to remove Muda;
Muda-tori improves both experience and
quality of life."

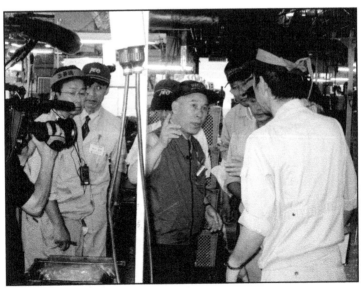

Photo 1: Yamada filming "Knock Down the Wall of
Common Knowledge – Factory Reform, the Post-Mass
Production System" at Sanyo Electric

1

ムダとりとはなにか？

What is Muda-tori?

Learning The Toyota Production System Directly from Mr. Taiichi Ohno

I first truly saw waste when I met Mr.Taiichi Ohno (the late, former Vice President of Toyota) in September of 1971. At that time I had just started my new job at the Gifu Prefecture Productivity Center after spending approximately two years as a newspaper reporter after graduating college.

I was in charge of training foremen when it was decided to invite Mr. Ohno, of Toyota Motors, as the main lecturer at a seminar organized by the Production Center. Mr. Ohno is the father of the Toyota Production System, which later had a great influence on the world's manufacturing industry.

It is said that the Toyota Production System was started from Mr. Kiichiro Toyoda's passion for improvement; when he declared in the post-war devastation that, "Productivity in the automobile industry will increase tenfold; In three years, we will catch up with the U.S." Mr. Ohno succeeded in his attempt to a tenfold level of productivity at Toyota in just 3 months, and it was at this point that he determined to devote his entire life to promoting Kaizen.

I was awakened to the benefits of Lean improvements by his seminar and eagerly asked him to show us his actual factory training. A number of us went to an automobile upholstery manufacturing company, where approximately 20 workers were sewing automobile upholstery for seats standing on one line. To our surprise, after one afternoon of training with Mr. Ohno their production improved tremendously and the production cycle moved smoothly, even after removing a number of workers from the production line.

They reduced the number of workers, seemingly by magic, by applying a complete elimination of waste through the use of the Toyota Production System. Could this really happen anywhere? The method was completely different from the control method I was taught by the Gifu Prefecture Productivity Center. It was a very powerful experience for me. I decided, at that moment, to learn to identify waste through the eyes of Mr. Ohno.

MAKING A NAME IN THE TEXTILE AND FURNITURE INDUSTRIES

The first time I put Mr. Ohno's Toyota Production System into practice was at a sewing factory in Gifu prefecture, which is known for its abundance of textile factories. When I looked at their production line, there was WIP accumulated randomly and it took about 14 days to make one pair of pants. Yet, after reviewing their Division of Labor and applying the multi-tasked worker method (assigning several processes to one worker), the delivery time that previously took 14 days was shortened to only 2 days in a time span of about 3 months.

In those days, using the Mass Production System, the cost of one ready-made garment was $5. However, if the garment was to be manufactured in 2 days, it could be handled as a semi-order-made garment and the cost of the garment could be raised to $10. The income of the company increased twofold in the same production cycle. After one year, the company paid $400,000 worth of taxes and suddenly appeared as the number one tax paying company in Gifu Prefecture, taking the industry by surprise. People began to pay attention to the company, asking, "How is it they are able to make so much money?"

Because of this success I wanted to promote the production system that I learned from Mr. Ohno further and I asked myself, "Which industry will benefit the most from a reduction in inventory?" As a result, I turned my focus to the furniture industry, which also experienced a great accumulation of WIP and inventory.

At one of the first companies within the furniture industry I worked with, they built a standard wedding gift set: a furniture set consisting of a Japanese-style chest, a Western-style chest, and a cabinet. Prior to implementing the Toyota Production System it took the company one month to make an entire set of the furniture; a Japanese chest at the beginning of the month, a Western chest in the middle of the month, and a cabinet at the end of the month.

In this way, the Japanese chest and the Western chest must be stored while the last piece, the cabinet, was manufactured. There was an abundance of waste in both their process flow and their inventory. To remedy this problem and eliminate waste I proposed that they make one full set of furniture in one day.

"If I could do that I would walk on my hands around the towns in Gifu," the company president commented; he did not believe it could be accomplished.

I commuted to the factory almost every day and worked through the processes with the employees to eliminate waste. To everyone's delight, we uncovered a way that the company could manage to make one set of the furniture a day. The company president's promise to walk around the towns in Gifu on his hands did not come true, but he was very grateful and my name became well known in the furniture industry.

OVERCOMING THE CHALLENGES OF WASTE ELIMINATION

I began receiving requests for consultation from major electrical manufacturers, one after another, as I continued to prove the benefits of waste elimination and factory reform. I worked closely with many large companies in Japan to eliminate wastes and improve their processes; such companies as Aichi Electric, Mitsumi Electric, Sony, NEC, Hirose Electric, Stanley Electric, Canon, and many more.

Among the factories I helped was a Sony job site where I gave training for one year in applying Muda-tori, or a Waste Elimination Management System. Waste is defined as anything within the process, people, or structure that is wasteful, including space, time, parts, people's potential, and more.

At Sony, starting in 1991, I succeeded in creating a usable space of 10,000 square meters in addition to helping create as many as 170 flexible workers in just one year. When you convert the number of workers into land and manpower costs, it is easy to understand that such waste elimination is worth millions of dollars in monetary savings at each respective location.

I also attempted to increase their productivity by applying the methods of space reduction (majime) and implementing a multi-tasked worker training program on the production line for their new products. To prove the benefits of the muti-tasked worker we tried the following:

A team of 10 workers was assigned to one assembly line and another team of 5 workers to a second line. In the first two weeks the productivity was better for the team of 10 workers, but after the two weeks the productivity per worker was higher for the team of 5. In addition, the quality of the products the team of 5 produced was greatly improved.

The Japanese word Majime has two meanings: distance/space reduction, and intelligence. The combination, however, means that it is intelligent to practice distance/space reduction. This is one of my favorite types of wordplay; where a word has the same sound but different meanings.

Thus as I continued to prove the effects of waste reduction my reputation grew, and in 1994 an article about Muda-tori appeared on the front page of the Wall Street Journal, introducing my name overseas as well.

In the training of Muda-tori, my Waste Elimination Management System, the first thing I see is the Shipping Department and then production job sites. Production schedules are managed by the most experienced workers, but many manufacturers outsource their shipping processes to external companies, who work in accordance with instructions given by manufacturers. Because these manufacturers often do not place much importance on shipping,

I frequently see manufacturers who are not aware of their customers' voices and situations. When I visit their factories I see many instances where products that customers want are not ready for shipping and unwanted products are piled up in their warehouses. In addition, it is also easy to find areas of WIP where workers are most concentrated within such companies. You can be almost 100% certain that there are areas of waste where people and things are the most concentrated. I focus on applying Kaizen in those areas first.

You cannot give a truly useful consultation if you must first get three years' worth of data on financial statements, analyze operations, and then go to a factory to start a Kaizen plan. Numbers and data are only shadows. The essence of how things truly are is all at a job site. You can only do factory Kaikaku through Muda-tori on the gemba, not from reports and paperwork. If a consultant or coach cannot identify problems on the shop floor by a quick glance, they are not a true consultant and you should be wary.

I believe that there is no use worrying about tomorrow when you cannot identify today's waste.

Wastes not only pressure organization's operations but also brings about serious resource and environmental problems, which also endangers the continued survival of humans.

LEARNING TO SEE FROM YOUR CUSTOMER'S POINT OF VIEW

Though my occupation is technically labeled "Management Consultant," often people more precisely define my job as a Factory Restructuring Consultant. My job is to visit companies around the country to help them improve their production lines, as well as educate supervisors and managers. I visit factories that are on the verge of breaking down; suffering from unprofitable business operations and an excessive amount of inventory. My job is to diagnose the problem and establish an accurate treatment plan; I do this by implementing a total restructuring of the factory. Through this I help them return to profitability and back to a condition where they can accomplish their goals.

Over the years I have helped well over 200 companies restructure their facilities, from layout to process flow, including many large enterprises that represent Japanese Industries such as Sony, Canon, and NEC Corporation.

In May, 2001, the Japanese broadcasting company NHK released a documentary film titled "Breaking the Mold—Factory Reform, the Post-Mass Production System." This film documented my efforts to restructure Sanyo Electric's Tottori Factory. (Sanyo later became affiliated with Panasonic). It is with an explanation of this film that I will begin to explain how factory restructuring happens and how I go about showing companies how to move beyond the non-sustainable Mass Production System into sustainable profitability.

The selected restructuring site for the film was their production line for mobile phones. The person in charge, who met with me to show me around the plant, first attempted to show me the material storage area, which is considered the starting point of a production process, as is typical for a factory visit. He wanted to guide me through their production processes in order; however, my approach is much different than the typical start to finish flow. The most important thing to know is where the products are shipped from, which is the closest point of contact with customers. So at my direction we headed to the shipping area, where products were stacked up in the finished goods storage area instead of being shipped out to customers.

> "How many trucks will be dispatched today?" I asked him.

> "We don't know yet," he replied.

> "That's no good! It is not good that someone who doesn't know today's sales volume is in charge here," I said loudly. "How can you determine the day's production schedule without grasping an idea of the shipping volume of your products? Without understanding the balance between shipping and production, you will simply create an excessive amount of products!"

The key to factory restructuring is managing the

process to eliminate the wastes of overproduction and inventory. In order to eliminate overproduction you must only produce the total amount of products that you can sell. If you produce 1,000 products and sell 1,000 products, then your inventory will be zero. In order to balance shipping and production it is necessary to understand the sales information about your products so that you can promptly respond to any situation.

IF YOU CANNOT READ IT FROM 10 FEET AWAY, DON'T DISPLAY IT AT ALL

Overproduction creates excess inventory; managers and employees in charge of a job site must understand this better than anyone else. In order to more clearly visualize this connection I suggested they display a large shipping control board on the shop floor that everyone could read from a distance. This control chart visually showed the workers, at a glance, how many of which products, made on which production line, were going to be shipped by which truck, to what destination. They were to display the chart at a location where everyone on the job site could see and record information on it correctly each time they saw it. This visibility meant that anyone, no matter if they worked in the department or were passing through, could easily see and understand the shipping information.

Visual control of information is necessary to ensure understanding throughout the organization. Instead of hiding the information away so that only managers with access to computers understand the information, it should be shared on an uncomplicated, easy to read display board that is accessible to everyone. One company that I gave a consultation to had 50-60 individual pieces of paper (invoices, work orders, etc.) flying back and forth around the factory for *each* order that was placed — between the receipt of the order and the delivery of the product. This method is a terrible waste of time and labor.

The first step to eliminating waste at a factory is for everyone at the job site to understand the status of shipping controls in real time, all the time. Basically, you should be able to read the control board from 10 feet away. If you cannot read it from 10 feet away people at the job site will not even attempt to read it. It is a waste, no matter how many control boards you make, if they are not read.

> ### *Yamada's Lean Lesson No. 2*
>
> "When you fail to use your will and wisdom at your work you fall into slavery.
> Are you spending eight hours a day doing only as you are told to do according to standard tasks and manuals?"

FACING THE ILLUSION: DIVISION OF LABOR DOES NOT EQUAL EFFICIENCY

After visiting the shipping department we proceeded to the production line, which was largely divided into three processes: assembly, inspection, and packaging. Sanyo Electric's Tottori Plant was currently working under the Division of Labor Production System; workers were lined up next to each other to assemble parts for mobile phones. Once one process was completed it was moved on to the next process, and so on. This method is considered to be a part of the traditional Mass Production System, which has been in use since the Ford era.

More than 40 workers were lined up along the total length of 164 feet of the production line assembling parts, inspecting, and packaging each unit one by one. I was surprised when I looked at the line.

"What on earth? How many items are stacked up here?" I asked.

Unfinished goods, better known as Work-in-Process (WIP), were piling up all along the production line. There was so much WIP between each worker it was difficult to tell where one person's area stopped and another started. The factory had all of the classic wasteful signs present when a company employs the use of division of labor.

Though the Division of Labor Production System appears to be logical, and may have contributed to production improvement when it was first introduced, there is a large error with the system—something the system doesn't take into account. Each worker's speed in performing a task is not the same. This difference between each worker's speed inevitably results in WIP between the workers, leading to a "reserve army of inventory."

Longer production lines and larger numbers of

workers proportionately increase the volume of WIP as well as number of areas that it can accumulate. More divisions of labor also increase the opportunity for WIP. It is only an illusion to believe that the Division of Labor Production System is logical and that it contributes to productivity improvements.

In addition, this system poses another problem. Suppose you want to stop the production line to change over to a new model of mobile phones; you cannot leave the WIP where it is, scattered along the production line. It requires massive amounts of time and energy to re-do a production line, making you unable to respond to consumers' demands and preferences. The old model must continue down the production line as long as there is remaining WIP to be completed, which needlessly increases the volume of dead stock.

If you cannot identify such things as overproduction and stagnation, there is no way for you to notice WIP. If you continue to be content with business running as it always has, you will never develop the ability to see waste. Factory restructuring is impossible unless you try to change.

THE ELIMINATION OF CONVEYOR BELTS

The elimination of waste at Sanyo Electric began by eliminating their conveyor belts. As described previously, their production line consisted of the three processes: assembly, inspection, and packaging. In the packaging process, the conveyor belt, the symbol of mass production, was moving as if it owned the place, therefore eliminating the conveyor belt was their first task. To tell the truth, conveyor belts had been viewed by everyone at the plant as "The King" of the process. Conveyor belts reigned over the mass production era and were still continuing to occupy the largest amount of space in many factories all across Japan. However, the role of the conveyor belt was already over—people just had to open their eyes and see it.

While conveyor belts were the tool for mass production, today they are only a relic of the past century, as we have entered into the new era of the High-Mix Low-Volume Production System. Once again, let's take a look at the job site from the point of view I just described.

Regardless of how fast humans perform a task the conveyor belt delivers products at its own pace, heedless of whether or not each process has been completed. Because conveyor belts do not work at the pace of the workers, workers must adjust themselves to the pace of the conveyor belt, which is not only inefficient but also does not give each worker enough time to complete their work and inevitably leads to poor quality. This is called the "reversed phenomenon." The job site was rather suggestive of Charlie Chaplin's movie "Modern Times" or the I Love Lucy episode "Job Switching." Thus inferior goods and WIP quickly accumulate throughout the factory.

Another disadvantage to using conveyor belts is that when one worker places a product on the conveyor belt it must travel a distance before another worker picks it up to work on it again. The product is WIP while it is moving on the conveyor belt; in the instance of Sanyo Electric, the distance between workers was 10 feet. Is the time and power costs to run the belt during the movement of materials not a waste?

Suppose we eliminate the conveyor belt and shorten the space between the workers to manually hand over the product to the next worker. Would that reduce the wastes of moving the materials, time (stagnation), and the cost of power to move the belt? We would not only save power consumption but also lighting and air conditioning costs by reducing the space, thereby reducing Sanyo's environmental impact.

As an example of this, at Canon I introduced the concept of space reduction: a worker would physically hand over a product or part directly to the next person. To do this we totally dismantled the conveyor belts and re-arranged the entire work space. Through the elimination of their conveyor belts at their domestic factories in Japan, Canon estimated that they reduced their CO_2 emissions by 6.6%.

It is this idea of shortening the space, the use of majime, between workers to enable them to hand products to each other that will minimize labor waste throughout the process.

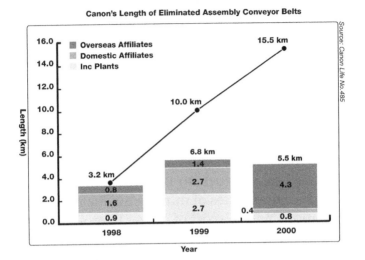

*Figure 1: Length of Conveyor Belt Eliminated in the
Assembly Department at Canon*

Canon's production reform movement started in 1997 at their Nagahama factory and eventually became a company-wide movement. The objective of the movement was to grow out of the conventional conveyor belt Mass Production System by introducing the Cell Production System. As a result of their efforts, Canon eliminated a total of 15.5 km (9.6 miles) of conveyor belts in 3 years. The company president's understanding and leadership were essential in accomplishing this goal.

> ### *Yamada's Lean Lesson No. 3*
>
> "Eliminating Muda is the desire to improve. You cannot see Muda without the aspiration for improvement each day, and there is no way to improve when you do not see Muda."

REFORMING THE ASSEMBLY LINE, YAMADA'S WAY

The next step was to reform the assembly line at Sanyo Electric. Let's review briefly the contents of the reform that I began with:

1. Eliminate the conveyor belt line for packaging.

2. Shorten the overall production line and the space between workers to reduce WIP accumulation as much as possible.

In addition to these two items, I came up with the following strategy to reduce waste even more:

3. Promote the multi-tasked worker method by assigning more than two tasks to one worker.

4. Apply One-Piece Flow to products.

5. Introduce the Single Stall Production System.

Item No. 3 above aims at reducing the number of workers in the process and number of occurrences of WIP by assigning multiple tasks to each worker. In the old production system each worker only ever repeated a single task.

To accomplish this I instructed the workers to learn the tasks of the workers directly next to them, thereby ensuring any one worker would be able to perform three persons' worth of tasks. This would also motivate the workers by giving them a challenge: to learn new tasks and skills. We can use this same thought process when it comes to cooking. Rather than making the same dishes week after week, I believe that if you challenge yourself to make different dishes, such as delicious French or hearty Italian, you will not only make your family happy but you will also find more joy in cooking.

Item No. 4, One-Piece Flow, means that a worker does not hand over a product to the next worker in the production line until that worker finishes his/her task, even if the first worker has completed their task. They also would not begin a new task until they had handed over that finished product to the next worker.

The most significant benefit of the One-Piece Flow method is that you can immediately identify where products tend to accumulate in the actual flow of the process and can assign workers accordingly to adjust the flow of the production line. In addition, if workers know the tasks of the workers next to them they could easily help each other complete tasks. Utilizing this production method, no WIP would accumulate between the workers.

THE CHALLENGES OF THE SINGLE STALL PRODUCTION SYSTEM

I decided to give Sanyo Electric another big challenge. They were to introduce the Single Stall Production System; item No. 5 on the list. You may not be familiar with the name but the Single Stall Production System is a production system in which one worker is in charge of all the processes of one product, from assembly to inspection and packaging. All of the parts and tools are placed around a worker, just like a Japanese festival stall[1] or a mobile taco truck, to ensure a smooth flow from process to process. In this method one worker is the master of the "stall" in the same way that a worker in a mobile food truck will take an order, turn to grab the ingredients necessary, quickly cook the food, then hand it off to the customer.

I had first tried this production system at NEC Nagano in 1993, which ended in success. The experiment at NEC was on their production line for word processors (computers)—basically electronic typewriters. In the reform of NEC's production line, I eliminated the conveyor belts and shortened their production line from 28 workers to 12 by applying the "space reduction" method previously described. To our surprise and delight, the productivity increased by 20% by applying this method alone. Efficiency increased in proportion to the number of

---

1   At a Japanese Festival Stall, one worker is the master of the "stall" and completes one product, similar to the way a shop owner of a Japanese festival stall cooks a piping hot fresh Okonomiyaki, a savory pancake, on an iron plate and wraps it and sells it to you.

workers reduced, in comparison with the Division of Labor Production System. In addition, the productivity increased again by 20% when we reduced the number of workers down to 5.

Next, we divided the workforce to attempt to have one person make one complete product. The result was just what I expected.

120 parts, which could create 65 different types of word processors, were placed at the stall for each worker. It took a total of 18 minutes for one worker to complete one word processor, starting from assembly through inspection and packaging. It took 24 minutes for 5 workers in the Division of Labor Production System to complete one word processor. The productivity increased 25% by applying the Single Stall Production System in comparison with the Division of Labor Production System. Today, the Cell Production System, which is similar to the Single Stall Production System, has been successfully adopted at many factories, including Sony where a small team of workers assembles each product.

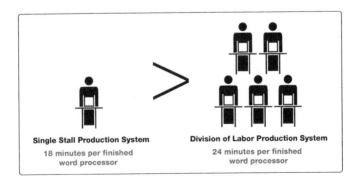

Figure 2: Division of Labor vs. Single Stall Production

At Canon they took the development of the Single Stall Production System even further and gave the name of Meister (a German word meaning master craftsman) to workers who mastered the skills of completing high quality products in a short period of time. Canon's Meister System gives pay incentives to workers in accordance with their skill levels, ranging from 3 (the first level to be achieved) to 1 (most knowledgeable of all the Meisters). By creating more Meisters, even the addition of 1, Canon is able to manufacture products more efficiently and with higher quality. As an added bonus, the workers' skill levels can also be more accurately evaluated this way.

The goal is not only to increase productivity but to encourage workers to engage their workplace. If the speed of a production line is constant, individual worker's efforts do not matter much and the worker is unable to contribute his/her ideas and efforts to productivity improvement. However, in the Single Stall Production System each worker's ideas and efforts are directly linked to the improvement of quality products and the worker can enjoy his/her craftsmanship when assigned to complete an entire product. It was through this example that I convinced Sanyo Electric to try the Single Stall Production System.

By minimizing hand and operation movements a product can be completed in a shorter amount of time than it originally took on a conveyor belt. Of course, one must always keep in mind that it takes time for workers to adjust to a new system. There was some anxiety at Sanyo Electric about whether or not one person could complete a whole product alone. I ventured into this challenge against some doubtful opinions about the possible outcome.

I felt confident from my past successful experiences at NEC Nagano, however as the first few days of the reform passed the speed of production proved difficult to increase. The workers tried hard to find ways to increase their speed and were constantly adjusting the height of their work benches and the areas where tools were kept. Eventually the workers got the hang of their tasks and, to our surprise, on the fourth day the production time was reduced to 7 seconds shorter than the conveyor belt system. It took only 200 seconds to assemble one mobile phone at this time. This was the moment when the Single Stall Production System overwhelmingly surpassed the conveyor belt and the appeal of the old production system.

Yamada's Lean Lesson No. 4

"Innovation is the achievement that allows more discovery and leads to more inventions for the future—it is never ending."

Photo 2: Single Stall Production at Canon

SAVING WORK SPACE AND ACHIEVING A FLEXIBLE MANPOWER SYSTEM

A large amount of space was left after eliminating the conveyor belts at Sanyo, and from that expanse of space we began to utilize the methods of "Making Use of Space" and "Making Use of Manpower." As the names indicate, it means to make the best use of both available space and manpower. By eliminating not only the conveyor belt itself, but also the excessive space needed for storing materials and inventory, we could free up a lot more space that could be put to better use.

It is important to understand that Making Use of Space means to make the best use of space that is created by eliminating waste. I would also like to mention here, to avoid any misunderstanding, that Making Use of Manpower is not the same as "restructuring" or "dismissing workers" by any means. The point here is to best utilize the now available workers, created as a result of shortening space, by training multi-task workers. Each company has different ways of utilizing such space and workers.

For example, we could assign a worker to support a department in need of additional workforce, or internally assign a worker to a process that was previously outsourced.

It is a manager's task and responsibility to come up with ideas on how to make the best use of their workers; for example, asking for workers' support to start up a new product line or business.

In the case of Sanyo Electric's Tottori Plant, there was a strong desire to keep the employment of about 3,000 workers. The company wanted to regain its strength in order to bring other production lines, at that time outsourced to China, back to the Tottori Plant. For this reason people listened to my advice to work together in their efforts. If a manufacturer's mission is to foresee new demands and continue to deliver useful and attractive products into the world, I believe that the strategies of Making Use of Space and Making Use of Manpower must become their strongest weapon in developing their next operational strategy.

KARAKURI

Many who have read this far may think that I am a person of anti-mechanization, however this is not true. I simply see an abundance of waste that is created by large, expensive machines. The wastes of Overproduction and Inventory are created by the Mass Production System and the amounts of large machinery (conveyor belts), which are automated and run at high speeds. This doesn't mean, however, that you can simply remove them from the production floor — you need to replace them with a new system and different machines. The new machines must be small, inexpensive in comparison, and serve the same purpose.

This new system must operate with minimal expense, both monetary and environmental, yet deliver a great impact. Instead of investing in machinery that costs tens of thousands of dollars which will turn out thousands of products that may not sell, it is important to use our creativity to make smaller machines that perform the same tasks without the cost and waste. Thus I came up with an idea, based on the Karakuri concept, which I proposed to Sanyo as the best method to eliminate waste from machinery. The idea is to make cheaper and simpler machinery internally that has the same functionality as that of the larger scale automatic machinery it will be replacing.

My idea originates from the clockwork mechanical puppets in the Edo era of Japan, which used wooden cogwheels and whale hair as the mechanism to create movement. The "Tea Serving Puppet," known as "Karakuri Giemon," is famous among those mechanical puppets. The Tea Serving Puppet's action are this:

A small boy carrying a tray of teacups appears from the corner of the room and serves teas to guests. After the guests finish drinking their tea and put the teacups back on the tray, the boy turns around and returns to where he came from.

I was amazed by the skillful movements of the puppet. While I gazed at the mechanism of the puppet, I noticed that the various movements of the machinery consisted of a combination of simple circular motion and reciprocating motion.

An idea flashed across my mind one day. "We can manually make our own machinery by applying the same principle," I thought. "We can devise wonderful machinery through the use of simple mechanisms."

The conventional machinery used at Sanyo Electric required electricity and air to run, and they needed large-scale equipment which consumed a lot of energy. The biggest benefit of Karakuri for Sanyo was that their new machinery could run manually or with a motor. This smaller machinery was not as complicated as the larger scale machines and they required far less power to run.

FROM $150,000 DOLLARS TO $5,000 DOLLARS

I would like to introduce one example of Karakuri in use at a large component manufacturer, Stanley Electric's Tsuruoka Plant. The target machine to replace assembled extremely small light bulbs. The conventional machine consisted of two turn tables, to carry the light bulbs, and several robot arms. After small parts were inserted in the light bulbs, the inspection was performed further down on the same machine. The cost of the machine was $150,000. It is understandable why the factory manager felt that mass production was the most optimal production system; a large machine such as this is prone to making hundreds of goods, one after another, by simply pressing a button.

> "Study the machine thoroughly to find areas of wasted movement," I told the manager. "And build a smaller, better machine."

After many weeks of trial and error by the research staff, a machine was created that could insert the small parts as well as perform lighting inspections by using only a small motor. The motion created from the combined motor, cam, and springs, without using the robot arms, was much more efficient. The size of the machine was about 1/27th the size of the larger one and the production cost was $5,000 Dollars — 1/30th that of the larger machine.

Normally, the market price of a machine is four times that of the material cost. For example, the selling price of a machine with the material cost of $15,000 would be $60,000. The manufacturing cost of the machine built by using Karakuri, can often be made for approximately half the material cost, or even as low as 1/30th of the material cost in extreme cases, as in the example I shared with you of the Stanley Tsuruoka Factory. As a result of its company-wide continuous Kaizen effort, the Stanley company managed to complete the tasks, which previously required 670 people, with only 450 workers.

The ability to see waste can lead to remarkable cost reduction.

It isn't unusual among the companies that I continue to guide with the Karakuri method to hold Karakuri Research Meetings to help one another develop a Karakuri machine. These groups are often very secretive about their work, but because they all have been work-

ing on the concept with me, they can get together to pool their creative energies together and complete a machine.

Yamada's Lean Lesson No. 5

"Don't think you have achieved something just because you are working late.
You are proven to have worked hard when someone else recognizes and evaluates your efforts."

Photo 3: Karakuri Machine

Yamada's Lean Lesson No. 6

"Make products that sell without effort. Discounting products only becomes necessary because of overproduction."

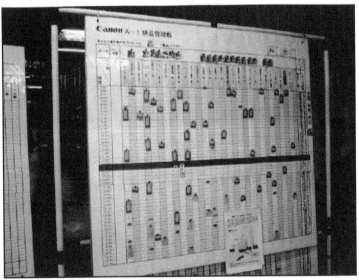

Photo 4: Production Board at Canon

2

脱大量生産宣言

ESCAPING FROM MASS PRODUCTION

DAWN OF MONOZUKURI—THE ART OF MANUFACTURING GOODS

The start of Monozukuri, or art of manufacturing goods, dates back to the French Revolution in the late 18th Century. The citizens, who had long been forced to live obediently under authoritative powers and religions, were awakened to the power that each individual possessed.

Each citizen began to understand what he/she needed in order to gain material wealth in an era when materials were scarce. They challenged Monozukuri themselves, not depending upon companies or organizations. In order to gain wealth it was necessary for each person to manufacture a product that was as uniform as possible, as efficiently as possible, and in as great a quantity as possible. To meet their needs various types of machinery were developed; the invention of machinery made it possible to repeat the same processes without having to rely on human or natural power. It was the dawn of the manufacturing industry.

Then came the Industrial Revolution, occurring during the 18th-19th Century, which began in the United Kingdom then spread across Europe, North America, and the rest of the world. Machine weaving replaced the conventional method of hand weaving through the power of the steam engine; thus the new textile industry started. Automation made mass production possible and the textile industry was the driving force, opening the road to the industrialized era that followed.

ORGANIZATIONAL CHALLENGES FOR ACHIEVING MASS PRODUCTION

The seed of mechanization that sprouted in England continued to grow and blossom in The United States, where they began the study of mass production. In the 1840's, Samuel Colt invented a system that separated parts production and the final assembly process, creating a batch production process. Years later the Taylor System of one person performing one task (Division of Labor) was proven to be most efficient through the Studies of Time and Motion, performed by Frederick Taylor and Frank Gilbreath. Following the studies, Ford invented the Conveyor System, during the early 20th Century, and the Mass

Production System was developed even further.

The introduction of the Mass Production System, when products were scarce, not only showed people the wealth that could be obtained from manufacturing but also created a new field of work. Called the Study of Operations, this emerging field contributed to the creation and development of organizations who utilized the Mass Production method.

It was also the U.S. that splendidly overcame the biggest domestic challenge of World War II: being the only country among the advanced nations to retain its industrial power without burning the country to the ground. It became the production base of the world's industrial products. As a result, the American Industrial Production and Study of Operations fields of study were recognized as the world standard.

How have we defined the manufacturing industry in the past? Manufacturing was about how to produce as many items as possible, as cheap as possible, and supply these products to the market. This creates satisfaction and happiness among the population because they are not lacking for supplies, which in turn increases society's respect for the large companies who provide for them.

This big company dream of being idolized and held in great esteem was realized through the Mass Production System. The leaders of the automobile society, GM and Ford, who produced some of the most popular automobiles, and the Japanese manufacturers such as Toyota and Nissan, as well as Toshiba and Hitachi, became "the symbol of the era" and they were viewed with respect. It was through many unskilled workers, the Division of Labor System, and the Conveyor Belt System that the realization of mass production and cheap supply was achieved.

Yamada's Lean Lesson No. 7

"If you do not react to problems you will never accomplish great results.
Unless you persistently try to identify hidden Muda you will not realize what you are capable of achieving."

CREATING A NEW APPROACH

This new system needed a new organization. Mass production and sales by the Division of Labor System prompted businesses to become structural organizations.

The larger an organization becomes, the larger the division will become among business owners, managers, supervisors, and the majority of workers who support the business at the bottom of the organizational structure. Organizations had transformed themselves into an authority, with management at the top.

Soon people shifted their focus to how to best climb up the organizational pyramid as efficiently as possible. As a result, even education shifted to follow this paradigm; seeking after authority and title. In order to become an executive of a large corporation people had to graduate from top universities. In order to enter the best universities, they had to select a high school, junior high school, and even kindergarten that were also considered best in class.

To make matters more frustrating, once a person managed to enter their desired company, after fierce competition, other hurdles must still be overcome. These new obstacles were often in the order of new employee education, followed by training for each department, and then training for each job title. The new employees who entered the company with passion for their work would spend days and nights competing with each other, and those who dropped out from the competition would become stuck, never to rise beyond the level at which they stopped advancing.

In the field of manufacturing, the larger an organization grows the greater the hierarchal competitiveness becomes and the more functional subdivisions of labor are created. To make one product the process involves the development department, production department, and sales department, each separated from the others and very few opportunities arise for direct discussions between the different departments.

The unfortunate reality of the manufacturing industry is that over the years organizational walls have become thicker and thicker and individual efficiency, as well as overall organizational efficiency, has become imbalanced. Because of this people began to talk quietly about what was dubbed "large company syndrome."

The time between development and sales (the production lead time) also became longer and more discrepancies began to occur between forecasted production volume and actual sales. Large inventories, which stemmed from the imbalances between production and sales, was the major cause of both price deflation and industrial destruction.

It is in the wake of the breakdown of the Mass Production System that we are working to create less wasteful, more customer-focused companies.

THE DECLINE OF MONOZUKURI

The development of industrial technology has achieved remarkable progress in the past 50 years. Only 50 years ago, no more than a handful of developed countries were able to manufacture the goods that we enjoy today. Scarce products were highly valued, increased people's desire to obtain the product, and raised the value of the products even higher, which in turn encouraged the development of mechanizations in order to make industrial production possible for any country. It was Japan that spearheaded this move to industrialization.

Japan imported machinery from The U.S., who was at that time the world's number one industrial nation, and applied their own innovation and techniques to produce goods. With their cutting-edge innovations, Japan used its cheaper manpower to export products back to the U.S.. "You get what you pay for" was a synonym for the earlier products made in Japan, describing the low quality of work. However, diligent Japanese workers succeeded in raising quality and standardizing mass production as a result of their efforts to improve technologies and productivity, and in addition introduced continuous Kaizen efforts on their manufacturing floors. This built the bulk of wealth during the high economic growth in Japan.

It is ironic that Japan is currently facing the same issues that the United States did; the reckless pursuit of wealth during a period of high economic growth in Japan resulted in the gradual loss of overseas competitiveness to China and South East Asia, who had cheap labor (said to be 1/30th of the labor cost in Japan). Japanese textile products, once renowned as second to none in quality around the world, began to lose production volume.

To go along with this, Japan has now completely reversed its position in the ceramics industry, from being a main contributing industry of Japanese exports to importing ceramics. It is not only the light industries that have changed, however. Even the production of automobiles and consumer electronics, once the star businesses that supported the wealth of Japan, are now moving their factories to China and South East Asia, seeking cheaper labor there. There appears to be no turning point now to change this trend. Products with the same manufacturing process and price are manufactured at similar production lines and processes elsewhere; yet, the wages of workers are ten times cheaper in China than in Japan. There is no way for Japan to win the price competition if they continue to compete on the same manufacturing level.

Muda-tori can help resolve both the issues of labor and production by reducing waste in every aspect of a business. This reduction of waste brings a greater sense of accomplishment and responsibility to workers to improve the process and discovering new ways to manufacture goods.

Aside from simply eliminating waste within the factory, Muda-tori will also help to eliminate the wastes that we are currently facing which impact our environment. 1.2 billion televisions and 500 million automobiles that did not exist 100 years ago are now flooding the earth. In a few years many of them will become trash and have nowhere to go.

The Japanese word "Mottainai" means a sense of regret concerning waste, when the intrinsic value of an object or resource is not properly utilized. For instance, when you purchase a product based upon an urge instead of a need — this is wasteful.

Yamada's Lean Lesson No. 8

"The focus today should be on quality of labor, not quality of products. If labor quality is improved, product quality will be assured. You only deserve more than an average salary if you do something above average—perform with better quality to achieve and receive more."

ESCAPING FROM MASS PRODUCTION WILL SAVE INDUSTRIES

The reason why Chinese products are strong in the market place today is, mainly, because they are cheap. Conversely, the reason why Japanese products are expensive is that there is no amount of productivity that can counteract their expensive manpower costs. The reason for low productivity is excessive Muda, or wastes, within the system. "Made in Japan" is being replaced in the U.S. with "Made in China," (As an example, Japan used to lead in the appliance industry, but now it is said that at least 30% of home refrigerators in the U.S. are made in China). In Japan, people have accepted the idea that the most efficient and productive method, in terms of worker productivity, is mass production and the use of conveyor belts. However, the time has come to change that notion.

As described in the previous chapter, the Mass Production System is inherently wasteful. Conveyor belts themselves are an extremely large waste. Industries will fall apart if they are unable to implement Muda-tori, or Lean practices, to eliminate waste. The conveyor belt demands humans repeat the same task monotonously without errors. It is the conveyor belt system that communicates to workers, "You only need to know and do this one task for the rest of your life." In that sense, I think that the use of the conveyor belt system clearly shows how organizations ignore the abilities of humans.

The conveyor belt system is wrong from an ergonomics point of view also. It is a system that completely ignores human psychology, physiology, and the potential inherent in every human. I think that the capabilities of humans, once they are placed in the right environment, will grow rapidly. The conveyor belt, however, deprives people of the most humane and essential abilities to be inspired and motivated: ambition and enthusiasm. We need to be aware of the evils of the Mass Production and Division of Labor Systems, which depend on conveyor belts.

Maximizing the use of People and Space Through Muda-tori

If you work on a manufacturing floor, try to eliminate your conveyor belt(s) as an experiment. You will soon find that a worker who previously performed only one task is now doing various tasks proactively and actively seeking out more efficient ways to work. The worker begins to use his/her brain and, as a result, his/her productivity will increase tremendously.

For example, in the case of Sanyo Electric, described in the previous chapter, the company reduced man-hours equivalent to 364 workers in a period of 5 months. Reduction of man-hour means, of course, the elimination of excessive workforce; they required fewer workers to manufacture the same product and could now use these workers to create new products and bring previously outsourced processes back to their main plant. The volume of WIP was reduced by a total of $4 million dollars in half a year by letting one worker perform more than one task, without the use of conveyor belts. Furthermore, the space that was needed for one process, once occupied by the conveyor belt, was reduced by as much as 6,800 square meters.

The historical approach, which became the "common knowledge" of the industry, was proven to be universally wrong because the phenomena of productivity increases without the conveyor belts was the same at all the companies I gave my consultation to.

It is a waste of human ability to force a worker into the framework and mindset of only utilizing a single skill. The first thing that organizations should do is to free themselves from the notion of mass production (or mass consumption). Each person's abilities will increase tremendously once they are freed from the framework of "single-skilled workers" and are led to the framework of "multi-skilled workers." Waste elimination invites the opportunity to use manpower and available space to the best of the organization's abilities. Muda-tori, the Waste Elimination Management System, is not, by any means, a cold blooded philosophy that stresses productivity alone. It is not a system that abuses the work force by prioritizing profitability either. It is a philosophy that values human potential and the pursuit of happiness.

Regarding Figure 3 on the following page:

Canon implemented Muda-tori to improve its production line. In 1998 they began practicing the Single Stall Production System and eventually introduced the Cell Production System, where more than one person may be working in a cell at a time. As a result, the company achieved a savings in space the equivalent to approximately 100,000 square meters in 1999 and approximately 150,000 square meters in 2000, totaling approximately 250,000 square meters. The company implemented a multi-skilled training program for 2,457 people in 1999 and 7,148 people in 2000, totaling approximately 10,000 people.

Making Use of "Space" and "Man" at Canon

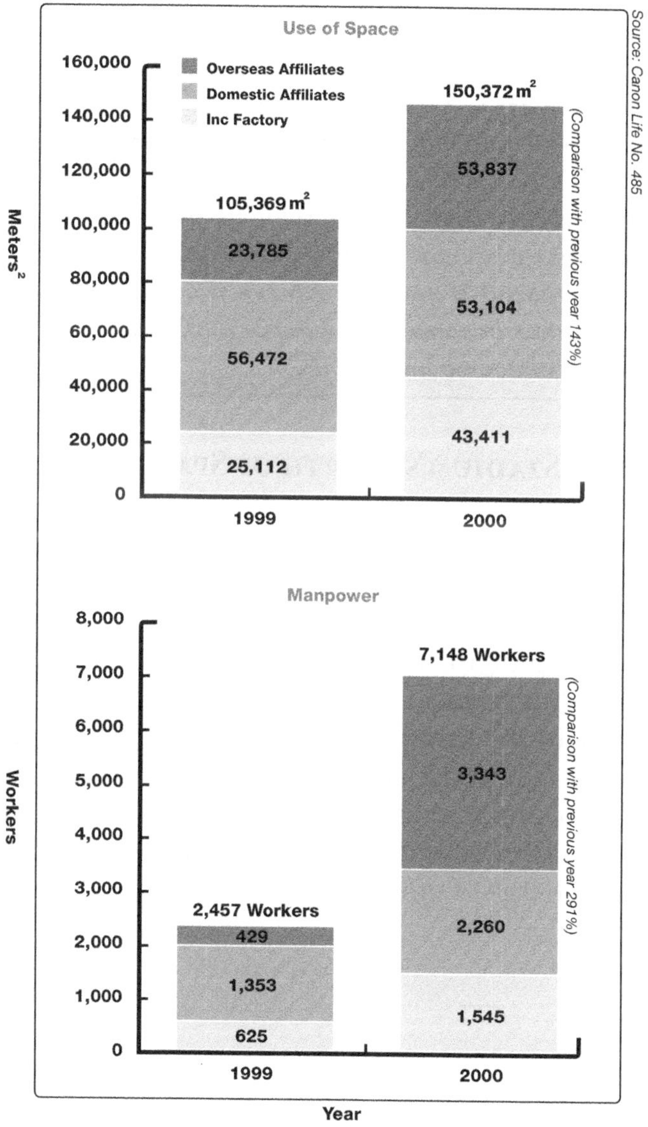

Figure 3: Making use of Space and Manpower at Canon

> ### *Yamada's Lean Lesson No. 9*
>
> "You are a true manufacturer if you can produce a high variety of more expensive products with as little workspace, as few workers, and least expensive equipment as possible.
> If you do that you will win customer satisfaction, whose quality of life you have increased. If you can achieve that, each worker becomes more important and their skills become invaluable.."

HALF A STADIUM'S WORTH OF SPACE WAS SAVED

In 1997, at Sony's Senmaya Factory, the following experiment was made:

A group of 10 workers was in charge of one assembly line (typical for the plant at that time). Each worker in the group assembled his/her own parts that the conveyor belt delivered. Of course, this wasn't a problem as long as each worker did his/her own job without a mistake because each worker was in charge of only one task.

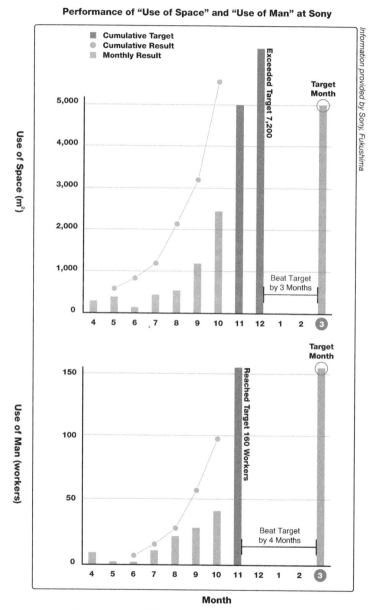

Figure 4: Use of Space and Manpower at Sony

Another group had only 5 workers and no conveyor belt. Each worker in this group assembled their portion of the parts and then manually handed the assembled parts over to the next worker.

For the first two weeks of the experiment, the speed of the group of 10 workers was faster than the group of 5. However, after around two weeks the situation reversed itself and the group that was manually delivering the parts to the next worker became faster, increasing the productivity per worker. In addition, the quality of the finished product was much better for the group of 5. The reason for this may be the increase in human empowerment, as experienced by companies in the previous examples.

Through this improvement at Sony's Minokamo Factory, a space savings of 10,000 square meters was realized in only one year as a result of Muda-tori. It goes without saying that everyone at Sony was completely astounded to learn that half the space of a baseball stadium had been wasted. The improvement also created 170 flexible, multi-skilled workers. If you add all of these improvements together it amounts to an annual cost of hundreds of thousands of dollars. This meant that much money was wasted during the era of the conveyor belt; that 10,000 square meters and 170 workers had been wasted at a single factory. If a company can find a good use of the newly created space and workforce, such as Sony encountered, it will no longer need to depend on restructuring.

SUPER MEISTER WHO DOES 70 WORKERS' WORTH OF WORK

Canon succeeded in the reduction of man hours equivalent to 7,000 workers in only one year (from 2000 to 2001) by implementing Muda-tori. They also removed over 9 miles worth of conveyor belts and uncovered 150,000 square meters worth of space.

As I mentioned in the previous chapter, Canon executed my recommendations very diligently. They then went above and beyond and introduced the Meister System, which aims to encourage multi-skilled workers who perform a wide range of tasks at a high skill level. The system was started when the company moved to the Cell Production System, in which one or more workers complete a process without the use of conveyor belts. The system requires workers to have a greater range of skills than they did under the conveyor belt system, which only required the workers learn how to do one repetitive motion. The Cell Production System adds indispensable human elements, such as intelligence and responsibility, to the process.

Canon's high-end large color copy machine, the CLC-5000, has apx. 10,000 different kinds of parts. It takes 14 hours to build the machine. In the past as many as 70 workers built them on a production line but it can now be built by one Super Meister. This is the ultimate example of a multi-skilled worker.

The Cell Production System and the Meister System create workers who are called Super Meisters. The workers learn the entire processes of assembling the most complex machines, described in the machine's 3,500 page assembly manual, in only 7 months by actually performing each task (learning by doing). The name of the Meister who produced the machine is proudly printed side by side with the manufacturing numbers on the completed facsimile and copy machines. The area each Meister signs says cordially, "I made this copy machine and guarantee its quality and output. It is the highest quality product. Please take good care of it."

This pride in their work leads to an increase in quality that benefits the company as well as the individual. The people who take this personal achievement to the highest level are designated Super Meisters. Canon assigns Super Meisters to various positions in the upper development divisions and the lower sales divisions, because of their superior product knowledge, to coordinate their development, manufacturing, and sales efforts. Because of this, Canon has succeeded in creating an ideal manufacturing organizational structure.

Muda-tori makes it possible to create a new multi-skilled workforce, which is the biggest asset for any organization.

NEC IMPLEMENTS THE CELL PRODUCTION SYSTEM

A manufacturing subsidiary of the NEC Group in Japan, called NEC Saitama, manufactures flip style mobile phones, and there are no conveyor belts anywhere in the factory. They operated under the typical Low-Mix High-Volume Production System; and since the company moved from the traditional conveyor belt manufacturing to Cell Production they have doubled their production volume in just half a year. There are about 40 groups of workers on the manufacturing floor, where teams of 5 workers function as an independent cell to assemble mobile phones.

The cost breakdown of a mobile phone is as follows: 90% parts and materials, 10% for labor and facility costs. Cell Production creates the biggest advantage for reducing the costs of the 10%, creating a more competitive cost structure.

In the conveyor belt system, production volume per one conveyor belt is limited; the addition of a conveyor belt is the only way to increase the production volume. However, in order to install a new conveyor belt (of a length just over 300 feet), it is necessary to expand the current facility, and in some cases build an entirely new factory. This naturally requires a considerable amount of capital and time. The Cell Production System, on the other hand, has the flexibility to increase production volume at anytime simply by increasing the number of cells and establishing a good procurement system for parts. The Cell Production System allows each worker to decide on their own production goals, which will challenged their abilities, and also allows those goals to be managed and tracked by the organization.

The current production volume at NEC Saitama per person is more than double what it was in 1999. In 1999 each person produced 50 units; currently each person creates more than 100 units and every month the number of units produced per person increases by 2%.

Yamada's Lean Lesson No. 10

"Muda-tori is possible if you try to finish 8 hours' worth of tasks in 4 hours a day.
You need to understand how the work needs to be completed in order to complete tasks in half the time—you must standardize the process."

LINE COMPANY SYSTEM OF MATSUSHITA ELECTRIC

Matsushita Electric created their own industry, centered around electronics, and promotes the Cell Production System at 55 out of their 117 domestic factories, under the umbrella of the Matsushita Group. The factories manufacture finished products such as AV equipment, information communication equipment, and large household electrical appliances.

In the conveyor belt system a certain volume is manufactured, posing a risk of excessive inventory when a sudden decrease of demand occurs. Nothing is more wasteful than excessive inventory. In the Cell Production System, however, adjustment of production in order to respond to changing market demands is easy. Easy adjustment means no waste and no inventory. Productivity increases without waste.

Matsushita Electric initially increased their productivity by 10% by simply removing conveyor belts and adopting the Cell Production System. Then the Kikusui factory of Matsushita Electric expanded their thoughts beyond Cell Production and created the Line Company System. In the Line Company System, a line of cells, consisting of 2 to 4 workers each, is considered to be one unit of operations, or a company within a company. The purpose of the Line Company System is to have each unit be in charge of its productivity as well as its actual profit. Each unit is projected to gain a 15% profitability increase, however in actuality they consistently exceed this target.

Muda-tori has proven itself to be effective enough that it changes how companies operate at the most basic level.

CREATING A HIGH PROFIT STRUCTURE THROUGH MUDA-TORI

There are many other companies that have turned their deficit operations into profitable operations as a result of Muda-tori under my consultation. There is a company named KOA who manufactures resistors, which had been in a deficit for 3 years after the

Plaza Agreement[1], but they quickly turned into a high profit company through the use of Muda-tori. Within 2 years their improvement was so great that they easily surpassed their competition in profitability and saw a great increase in their company's stocks.

Mitsumi Electric is another company who quickly turned their balance sheet from the red to the black. The old Mitsumi Electric had considerably lower earnings compared with its competitor Alps Electric. After 3 years, however, the company reversed the situation.

Stanley Electric increased its sales volume by as much as 15% and its earnings doubled. Of course, because of this the company's stock price jumped up as well.

Tostem, a manufacturer of metal-framed sliding doors, followed the same path as Mitsumi Electric. During the home building boom of the 1980's, the company adopted the High-Mix Low-Volume Production, also known as Build to Order, (creating 400,000 parts used on metal-framed sliding doors) without engaging in Factory Automation, while at the same time lowering their cost to profit ratio. As a result, the company emerged at the top of their industry, even over YKK who had held the top position for years.

---

1   The Plaza Accord or Plaza Agreement was an agreement between the governments of France, West Germany, Japan, the United States, and the United Kingdom, to depreciate the U.S. dollar in relation to the Japanese yen and German Deutsche Mark by intervening in currency markets. The five governments signed the accord on September 22, 1985 at the Plaza Hotel in New York City.

There are many more examples like these in a wide range of industries, from automotive to apparel and furniture, as well as company size, from small family businesses to large global organizations. This shows that Muda-tori can bring improvements and high profit structures to any type of business, no matter the industry.

An important point to understand is that waste elimination is not a temporary business improvement structure. An organization can continue to maintain its high productivity only if it correctly understands how efficient production can be made by eliminating conveyor belts and changing to a multi-skilled worker paradigm. The improvement is then sustainable because the changes take place in the minds of managers and employees.

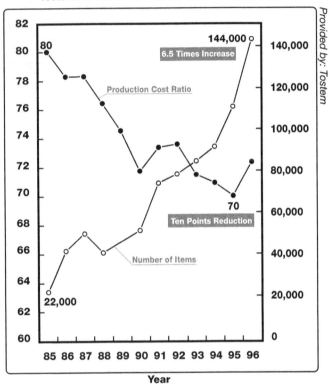

Figure 5: Production Cost Ratio and Product Count at Tostem

The old "common knowledge" tells us that increasing the number of items will increase the cost ratio with it. However, cost ratios will decrease even when the number of items increases if a company implements a High-Mix Low-Volume Production System. This production system eliminates the waste of overproduction, and through managing goals will increase production, as well as promoting the use of Karakuri.

> ### *Yamada's Lean Lesson No. 11*
>
> "Have the courage to be critical of yourself and your own work. Ask yourself, 'Is what I am doing now adding value?'
> Use this courage to identify wastes in your work and on the shop floor."

MUDA-TORI IS YOUR CHANCE TO MOVE FORWARD

There are some companies among those I have consulted whose high profitability was only a temporary thing. Instead of continuing the new ways I taught them, they returned to their old conveyor belt system and, without exception, each of the companies returned to their previous unprofitable condition.

It is not easy to change a production system. Without a change of mindset by management it is difficult to change an organization's structure. Stanley Electric has a superior structure now but it took the company 4 long years, after management finally shifted its mindset, before its earnings turned profitable. In my experience, it takes at least 3 years to change the mindset of an organization. During this period of change, I will visit production sites many times and persistently repeat the training we have gone through whenever I find Muda. Without doing so, the areas/departments I am brought in to change are the only areas which transform; other areas would remain the same, to the detriment of the entire program.

There are also some instances when a group of managers, who were once very enthusiastic about the improvement of their production sites suddenly change their attitudes and become uncooperative. This shift in attitude happens after a change takes place in their management structure.

Internal struggles for power often prevent an organization from improving itself.

For such organizations, I often must become the driving force for change myself. In these cases I will skillfully lead the management team and be the motivation behind improvements. This has the benefit of avoiding confusion and resistance to change, because I am the sensei they have hired to guide them.

On the other hand, if management leads themselves, I become the authority. Using my authority I carry the right to eliminate or restructure people so as not to slide back into an unprofitable and confused state. I do not have to do this often, but on occasion I run across companies that require such strong measures.

Change does not happen over night, so you must devote yourself 100% and believe this is your last chance for survival.

THE COMPLETE ELIMINATION OF MUDA IS THE FOUNDATION OF TPS

When the Low-Mix High-Volume (Mass Production) production era moved into the High-Mix Low-Volume production era the Toyota Production System was developed and my honored teacher Mr. Taiichi Ohno received the world's attention. The principle philosophy of the Toyota Production System is the complete elimination of waste. In English, the essence of the Toyota Production System is translated as "maximum value with minimum waste."

The Toyota Production System is supported by two pillars: Just-in-Time and Jidoka. Just-in-Time is the concept of supplying necessary goods, in the right amount, and only when the goods are needed. We need to prevent opportunities for waste to spread, therefore we need to reverse the direction of the conventional production flow, a process supplying goods to the next process. In Just-in-Time, the necessary goods are received from the previous process, in the right amount, when the goods are needed. No problems occur in this process so long as the exact quantity of a specific item is clearly indicated. This is established through the utilization of Kanban.

The other pillar, Jidoka, is also called "automation with human intelligence" because it has an automatic stopping device attached to a machine. This automatic stopping device (Poka-Yoke) prevents the occurrence of defects and allows a person to operate more than one machine at a time. Just-in-Time creates teamwork between operations and Jidoka makes each person more valuable because they can operate more machines and are more highly skilled.

Andon Signals, built into automatic machines, are particularly effective at creating awareness among the workplace. The Andon that Mr. Ohno invented has a mechanism that signals "I stopped the line" any place where a worker stops the line when they encounter a delay or failure in the process, and creates a sense of independence and responsibility. Through the use of these tools we can say that the Toyota Production System, targeting a complete elimination of waste, is a methodology that promotes an individual's sense of ability and technical skill and increases teamwork among individuals.

Yamada's Lean Lesson No. 12

"Anyone can criticize deficits in an accounting book, but the real problem is that people are unwilling to admit they are part of the problem. The willingness to fix problems and admit that you need to change is required in order for a company to change."

THERE ARE REALLY ONLY 3 WASTES

What are the wastes I am talking about on the shop floor? First of all, we can define waste on manufacturing floors as "various factors that don't add value and only serve to increase production costs." The Toyota Production System lists the following 7 Wastes:

1. Muda of Excessive Production (Overproduction)

2. Muda of Waiting (Delay)

3. Muda of Transport (Transportation)

4. Muda of Processing by itself (Extra Processing)

5. Muda of Inventory (Inventory)

6. Muda of Motion (Motion)

7. Muda of Defects (Defects)

I had some questions about these wastes, however. For example, Overproduction can be unclear on a manufacturing floor. At what point is production considered excessive and therefore wasteful?

After examining the companies who I gave my consultations to, I began to realize that there are truly only 3 wastes which affect both machines and people. As a result I started considering the following 3 as the true wastes:

1) Stagnation

2) Transportation

3) Motion

Stagnation is a new, very encompassing concept which accounts for such wastes as idle or underutilized machinery and the accumulation of materials and finished goods. This accumulation forces people, information, and machines to wait before they can be used or processed. You begin to see waste by recognizing and thinking about how you can reduce stagnation. Once you see stagnation, ask "Why?"

(Why is there stagnation?) 5 times and you will begin to uncover the root cause of the waste.

The waste of Transportation occurs when no value is added to a product by the materials being moved or transported from one location to another. For example, when a final product is transported from one side of a building to another before waiting to be shipped to the final customer.

The waste of Motion is caused by excess movement. For example, if a worker is having to reach to grasp a part to use in assembly, that movement is waste. In order to standardize processes, you must teach workers to recognize the waste of Motion so that they can eliminate the waste. Without this you cannot achieve optimal standardization.

For example, if you move parts from the right side to the left side of your workbench, the loss of 2 seconds per part you move accumulates to a total loss of hours. My advice is for parts or materials to not leave your hands once you receive them. 20 centimeters of a finger motion can lead to a loss of seconds in no time, and hours if nothing is done to remove the waste.

Standard work is the base for improvement, similar to practice in sports. As you continuously improve, your standard work improves. Once you have developed good standard work processes you will be able to train workers to see and eliminate wastes and they will be able to add true value to their work.

The workers I value the most on a manufacturing floor are those who believe that every motion must be value-added movement and who strives to remove all non value-added movements.

SWITCH TO THE MINDSET OF A HUNTER-GATHERER

At the time of the oil crisis in Japan people fiercely scrambled for such basic items as toilet paper and detergent. They rushed to the stores to stock up on these items, even though they must have had enough stock to last for a few weeks. It may be that they felt safer simply by having as much as possible in their possession. This is the mindset of the agricultural people, who never knew when they might face a disaster because what they are dealing with is nature, so they wanted to stock as much food as possible in order to survive whatever was thrown at them. Perhaps this mindset is still ingrained in our society, even though there is no longer a reason to horde supplies in such a manner.

There are many managers who feel unsafe without materials, WIP, and products in stock. However those materials, WIP, and products will become dead stock no matter how much is stored if there is no demand for them. In other words, they become a huge, unnecessary waste. The most rational way to avoid this is to procure only necessary things, when they are needed, and in the necessary amount.

This is the same as the mindset of the hunter-gatherer people and their lifestyle. For these people, hunting exists as their sole purpose; they hunt for what they need, when they need it. Therefore, they are careful about eliminating all wasteful items, clothing, and more so that they can move around easily and follow herds.

Managers must quickly switch to the paradigm of "Hunter-Gatherer" from that of "Agricultural People."

In the mass production and mass consumption era, the agricultural paradigm could sufficiently handle most situations. However, in today's High-Mix Low-Volume production era, such a paradigm cannot be accepted. **We are moving from the era of "manufacture and sell" to the era of "manufacture what you can sell."** An organization must become Lean by eliminating wastes to improve itself and create a stronger structure. To achieve this, managers' awareness must be adapted.

Yamada's Lean Lesson No. 13

"The slowest worker's pace is the fastest Mass Production can run.
Mass Production means providing the lowest quality of goods to people around the world in the largest quantities."

INCREASE PRODUCTIVITY WITH PRODUCTION VOLUME DROPS

Mr. Taiichi Ohno once said, "There are hundreds of people in the world who can increase productivity or efficiency by increasing production volume.

There are many such foremen at Toyota too, but there are only a handful of people in the world who can increase productivity when the production volume is decreasing. The more people who are capable of doing just that, the stronger an organization's structure will become."

For example, in today's economy China is rapidly expanding, and productivity and efficiency will increase no matter who leads a company's operation. They are following in the same footsteps Japan did during its rapid economic growth, and so the Chinese economic power will continue to grow. Japan, however, is now experiencing very low economic growth and cannot continue to manufacturing on the same stage as China, utilizing mass production. Production costs in Japan are simply higher than in China, no matter how you look at it.

What is required to out-perform China is to transform organizational structures to those that can increase profitability and productivity while continuing production that meets the demands of customers, who continue to spend less. Moving a production base overseas does not provide a fundamental solution, even if the cost of manpower is cheaper overseas. It is only a temporary solution that endangers the future and may lead to de-industrialization and weakened international competitiveness.

What is needed for today's organization is a complete elimination of waste and the maximum use of people and space. Organizational structure is strengthened when waste is eliminated.

There is no future for companies who do not strive for the elimination of waste.

MUDA-TORI IMPROVES YOUR QUALITY OF LIFE

Taking a long-term perspective, we must create a system that enables manufacturers to make a profit by manufacturing a product consumers will use throughout their entire life. For example, you can normally use automobiles for 10 or 15 years, however, automobile manufacturers repeatedly change and advertise new models to prompt consumers to trade their vehicle in and purchase the new models as quickly as possible. Regardless of how long an automobile can last, auto manufacturers make money hand over fist by prompting consumption. As another example, mobile phone and personal computer models are changed as rapidly as every few months.

I worry we will not be able to maintain a healthy, long-term global environment if new products are continuously manufactured and supplied as they are today. Our natural resources and how we supply energy to manufacture goods will run out. In order to avoid the worst-case scenario, I believe that we must quickly bring society back to a state where companies benefit from consumers using their products throughout their entire life, which in turn will benefit the consumers. I believe that now is the time for all businesses and business administrations to think seriously about building such a system. Otherwise, the earth will degrade within this century to become a place where no human can survive. It is a dreadful prediction of the future, but it is by no means fiction. The critical moment is just around the corner.

If the Chinese economy grows at the same rate as Japanese economy once did, the earth will certainly fall apart. If China, with a population 10 times larger than the population of Japan, were to rush into mass production and mass consumption mode, like Japan did, it is easy to calculate how fast the environmental destruction will progress.

We must stop the vicious spiral of producing goods to make money, at the expense of the environment, and making money to buy goods. We must completely eliminate waste in order to stop that destructive cycle. One waste will surely create another waste, which in turn will create more. That is why we must work very hard to eliminate waste altogether. When everyone is aware of Just-in-Time principles waste will disappear from society and even from the way we live of our lives.

Muda-tori saves not only production floors but individuals, organizations, societies, and even the earth itself.

Yamada's Lean Lesson No. 14

"A true leader is a person who understands the organization's purpose and identifies and recognizes who the followers are. A true leader will recognize what skills, knowledge, and motivation workers need to achieve that purpose."

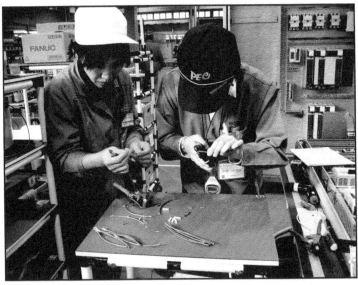

Photo 5: Sony Workstation Experimentation & Training

3

ムダとりを成功させる経営とは

MANAGEMENT THAT MAKES MUDA-TORI SUCCESSFUL

ONE MOUTH AND TWO EARS

One thing I have come to understand clearly during my years as a consultant is that an organization will go under if its supervisors and managers do not lead their employees well. Without good management to place responsibility on workers, workers will not seek to change for the better and the morale toward improvement will dramatically decrease. Low morale leads to workers who have little to no energy, and without this vital energy the company cannot change.

A manager for such an organization usually makes excuses such as, "You know the economy is not improving at all," or "We don't improve because of my employees." The employees in turn say, "It is because our boss is incompetent." They are laying the blame on each other. I think that shifting the responsibility on to others is the biggest evil in the Division of Labor System. Such a company will end up in failure.

A recent trend to combat a lack of improvement or productivity is for large companies to outsource their unprofitable departments as a part of their restructuring scheme. If managers are made aware that they are responsible for the department's poor business performance, they would not outsource their departments but work to fix them. The reason behind outsourcing unprofitable departments may be that the managers think that their subordinates are the ones to blame and not management itself.

I can hardly tolerate large companies who close down their facilities and let go of their employees. The president of such an organization would never do this if he believed that he is responsible for the unhealthy operations. The reason that a president will close down his company is because he believes that his subordinates are the reason for the company's failure, not himself. As soon as he realizes that management and the management structure is the problem it becomes a problem that can be solved and a challenge that the company will be able to overcome.

It is clear that a company full of self-righteous people will quickly fall apart because everyone believes their way is the correct way and will not stop to listen to anyone else. I want to believe that if people have a willingness to honestly listen to other people's opinions, they will be able to understand how to work together to change for the better. When I go to a manufacturing floor, I always ask the workers there, "Why are you doing things this way?" At first they may have their guard up or be reluctant to answer my question, but often they will quickly begin to voice their true opinions. From there we begin to see problems clearly. People only need to have patience to listen.

When I was a small boy, my mother used to say, "We have one mouth and two ears. Do you know why? Our body tells us to listen to two things before we say one thing. So if you do not listen to other people's opinions, you'll become useless." A company is in a terminal condition if the managers do not listen to their employees opinions. There is no future for such a company.

Listen to two things before saying one thing.

GET TO KNOW A COMPANY BY LOOKING AT ITS CUSTOMER CONTACT POINT

You can tell if a company's operations are going well or not by looking at its customer contact point. It is immediately apparent if the company is treating its customers well when you look at the expressions and attitude of the receptionist and the people in charge of shipping. Here is one simple example:

Operations at department stores are becoming more difficult because they are not treating their customers well. When I was a college student, sales persons at department stores had pride in treating their customers well. "Welcome to our store!" they greeted their customers courteously, showing the pride of working at a good department store. Working at a department store was even a prestige for many people.

Today, however, this pride in their workplace is gone as they have begun to treat their customers in the same manner as a supermarket. In order to be competitive to supermarkets, which now sell a variety of goods at low prices, department stores are simply hiring cheap labor to cut their costs. This results in poor customer service and employees who no longer care about their workplace.

It is the same way with banks. When I go to a bank, the first thing I must do is wait in line. Customers receive no greeting and are left waiting. If you wish to withdraw money from your account by an ATM, instead of standing in line at the bank, you are penalized and charged money, which often accumulates to more than the interest you might earn in a year from a savings account. Banks do not treat small citizens well, those who entrust and save their money with them, but they do treat large organizations, who have large loans with them, very well. There are no other businesses that treat their customers as badly as this; it is no wonder that banks are going under.

> ### **_Yamada's Lean Lesson No. 15_**
>
> "The Principle of Manufacturing "Don't produce items that don't sell" has been overshadowed by the idea of abundance. One thing that is overly abundant is information, which results in forecasting based on something other than true needs.
>
> This concept is embodied within agriculture as "Hosaku Binbo", meaning the impoverishment of farmers despite a bumper harvest."

DEVOTE YOURSELF TO THE ART OF MONOZUKURI

Nobody knows what kind of society is forthcoming after the collapse of the capitalistic society, however, it is certain that capitalism will come to end sooner or later. Today, monetary exchange amounts to 50 times that of material exchange. Furthermore, people are now making a living off of exchanging money with money, instead of exchanging goods for money. It is obviously an abnormal society, and such an abnormal society is destined to collapse sooner or later. Such a collapse is just around the corner, no matter which country is the first to go under; The U.S. with a huge trade deficit or Japan who is struggling with a budget deficit.

Japan, particularly, is in danger as it has forgotten entirely about the art of manufacturing. There are very few young people now who want to pursue a career in agriculture or get a job at a manufacturing company and work hard on a manufacturing floor.

Of course, some people may work on a manufacturing floor when they first start working at a company, however, the current condition is such that there are very few people who try to find the joy in manufacturing and master the skills as a professional. People will soon forget about manufacturing jobs altogether.

I am concerned about the future of Japan if it were to forget the manufacturing base that once built the strength of the country, allowing it to become an economic power in the manufacturing field. It seems to me that even the survival of the country in the 21st Century is doubtful.

I believe that each worker should have the experience of making an entire product, instead of working in the environment of mass production, so that they can remember the meaning of true manufacturing. People become livelier when they find pleasure in their work. It is easy to understand how people become more engaged, active, and passionate about their work when each individual is making a whole product in the Single Stall Production System, like the examples of Canon's Meister System and Sony's Cell Production System. This is the starting point of manufacturing. When there are motivated people around you, you become motivated to tackle your work more proactively as well. Morale as a whole is elevated. I believe that companies should devote all their energy into manufacturing instead of relentlessly chasing after company stocks.

Mr. Ohno said, "A product that comes out of a difficult situation, as a result of your hard thinking and wisdom, will become a truly acceptable product in the world." In that sense, now is the time for manufacturers to focus on creating superior products that are truly acceptable in the world.

HAVING THE COURAGE TO NOT PRODUCE

Why do we still continue manufacturing goods when goods are flooding the marketplace? Many manufacturers truly believe that the more goods they produce the more profit they could make. They feel reassured by introducing new facilities, one after another, so that they may continue increasing their production volume. They have no idea how to manufacture the goods that are desperately sought after, instead they manufacture goods that are found everywhere. Who wants to buy a product when the supply of the product is much more than the demand?

Products are not simply sold because they are cheap. When the quality of a product is superior and the supply is low, its value increases and sells well even if its price is high. Unfortunately, manufacturer's successful experiences during the Mass Production era and their knowledge of how consumption worked at that time are preventing them from realizing the differences of today.

What manufacturers need to be able to understand is that from an operational point of view stopping production imposes much less of a burden than piling up massive amounts of inventory. Production requires raw materials and generates warehouse cost and taxes, however, only the minimum manpower cost is required if you stop a production line.

Some companies that I worked with stopped their production for over a month. During that period the employees cleared weeds and tidied up around their factories. Despite the stopped production, sales were normal and orders were able to be met because their enormous amount of inventory was enough to last through their non-production time. This lead to receiving more cash than usual from sales because they were not having to pay for the cost of materials and electricity necessary when the production lines were moving.

When I visited Canon's facilities in Taiwan, I suggested to the company president that they stop their production line. He was worried about what would happen but he dubiously followed my advice. Later he confessed to me, "To tell the truth, I was worried that we might fall into a deficit, but that did not happen. I finally understand!" The surprise of not falling into a deficit even when production is stopped comes only after you experience it. You can overcome your common knowledge through actual experiences. Manufacturers should be freed from the misperception that they should continue manufacturing at any expense. Instead, they should develop a strategy that can respond flexibly to real situations. It is necessary for manufacturers to have the courage to *not* manufacture.

> ### **_Yamada's Lean Lesson No. 16_**
>
> "Creating an organizational culture that is able to change and adapt is more important that having an abundance of resources.
> An organization's strength is built upon this adaptable culture."

MANUFACTURING PRODUCTS THAT WORKERS ARE PROUD OF

According to the statistics of Gifu prefecture, my home, the volume of trash has increased 2 ¼ times in the past 10 years. The largest portion of trash is plastic bottles, which is understandable since just a few decades ago there were no plastic bottles at all. Some of the goods in the trash were bought because they were cheap, or the purchaser was bored, and were quickly thrown out by the people who bought them. The fact is that society as a whole is treating goods wastefully. As a result, the volume of trash continues to increase, leading to environmental destruction.

Taking the consumers' point of view, you may think that it is up to the consumers whether or not to throw away the goods because it was the consumers who bought it. However, how would your thinking change if you adjusted your viewpoint to that of the manufacturer, or person in charge of production?

Workers must ask themselves, "Have I been working hard to produce goods that are so easily thrown away?"

This is a very disappointing thought and is certainly no way to increase the morale of workers. An employee's attitude toward work will consistently degrade when they are told to create cheap goods that no one wants. Monozukuri holds no meaning if the morale of a company is severely decreased, especially when the company is engaged in a race to the lowest price of goods to be competitive. I believe it is a very dangerous idea to produce anything for the simple reason that a company believes they can sell the items. Managers should introduce a company-wide change so that shop floor workers become proud of what they do as well as what they produce.

CRAFTSMANSHIP AND MASTER SKILLS ARE THE BEST WEAPONS IN A SLOW ECONOMY

There were once craftsmen and artisans in Japan who possessed superior skills, respectfully called "Takumi." They made unique products with their refined skills and many people supported them and took pride in purchasing their work. The Takumi gradually disappeared as mass production and mass consumption became the dominant marketplace trend. The number of true craftsmen and Takumi is on the decline in the field of traditional arts and crafts as well, and more and more imitations are spreading.

Imitations lack the ability to produce a feeling of attachment because they have no unique characteristics nor do they have the soul that handmade products have. You naturally feel attached to a product made by a real craftsman, who painstakingly poured his/her heart and soul into its creation. If you feel attached to such a product you want to treat it well and use it for a long time. A gentleman by the name of Mr. Taichi Sakaiya, whom I met recently in a magazine interview, told me that he has used one bag for over 20 years; he has repaired the bag 4 times in order to continue using it. This is the kind of attachment that artisan crafted items foster.

Throughout the world companies have been moving to factory automation while ignoring the existence of valuable, highly skilled craftsmen. Isn't it about the time we move back the era of the Takumi once more?

It is in this golden age of computers that people are looking for unique products in which they can feel the warmth and personality of products, created by highly skilled craftsmen. The joy people receive in buying a product made with soul is greater than you can imagine. Highly skilled workers with a lot of experience on manufacturing floors, who take pride in being a craftsman, are an easy target of a company's restructuring scheme. However, it is a big mistake to remove the creativity from these people. Machines can be exchanged but craftsmen cannot.

There are many companies who make massive investments in facilities and equipment to produce excessive products because they think their products will sell. As a result, because they are creating products without paying any attention to what their customers actually want, the companies go bankrupt. It is not automation that will save manufacturing companies but the superior skills, and a touch of handmade warmth, of craftsmen.

There is no future for companies that abandon the superior skills of people under the name of restructuring. The only companies that can continue to grow steadily, even in a slow economy, are those that cherish higher quality skills and craftsmanship.

Yamada's Lean Lesson No. 17

"Companies often evaluate their organization by profitability not by the commitment of employees. Changes in profitability will only change if the organizational mindset changes. True results can only be achieved by changing individual mindset."

BIG COMPANIES NEED AUTONOMIC NERVES

The human body is very well made. When you see a delicious looking plate of food in front of you, more saliva is secreted. When you exercise, your heart beats faster to send fresh blood throughout your body. Without waiting for instructions from your brain, your body automatically adjusts itself. These adjustments are made through the body's autonomic nerves.

It is often said that companies are like living creatures. If so, something like humans' autonomic nerves are necessary for companies, too. A system is necessary for departments or employees to respond to changes quickly without having to wait for instructions. In today's fast paced world, you will lose the competition for your survival if you must constantly wait for instructions every time a problem is encountered. Business opportunities slip away from you while you are issuing paperwork and writing schedule changes. The larger a company gets, the longer the time it takes to get orders and instructions through the entire process and for this reason it is necessary to develop a system that is equivalent to the autonomic nervous system of the human body.

How do we accomplish that? By deeply imbedding the Just-in-Time philosophy throughout the organization and by implementing the rules of Kanban thoroughly. I have touched upon Kanban before, but I would like to explain further here. Kanban is a card on which information is written, such as production instructions for the previous process to replenish the parts that were used. The card shows the product name, product number (SKU), pre-process name, post-process name, quantity, and storage location.

Role of the Kanban

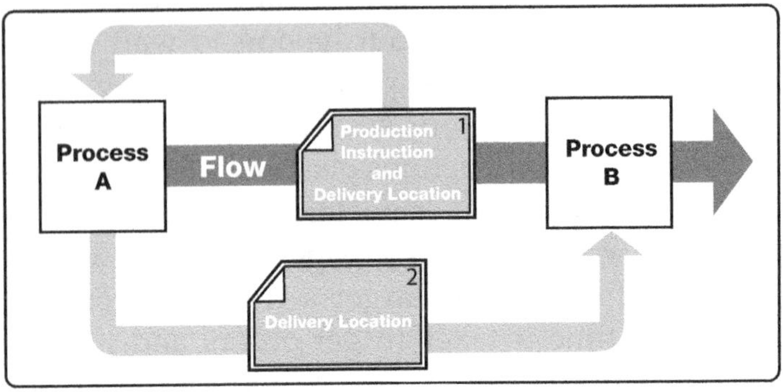

Figure 6: Role of the Kanban

The card attaches the necessary information directly to parts and WIP so that there does not need to be a reliance on paperwork, which can be easily lost or scattered. The Kanban is removed after one process is complete and ready to move on to the next process and placed where it will be seen by the previous process. The removed Kanban becomes an instruction to the previous process for replenishment of items that were used. This reduces the wasteful manufacturing of goods because if there is a delay in one process no Kanban is circulated and the entire line slows down.

Kanban has four important functions:

1. Suppress the waste of overproduction.

2. Convey information, such as receiving information and production instruction.

3. Act as a visual control tool.

4. A Kanban tool.

You can tell what, how much, and at which department the products are being made by looking at a Kanban. It is clear to each department, with one glance at the Kanban, how they should respond to changes without waiting for instruction from their supervisor. With this method in place we can easily say that Kanban is a brilliant autonomic nerve system.

In order to implement Just-in-Time and Kanban efficiently everyone needs to be constantly thinking about what is presently needed. I believe that the larger a company gets, the more autonomic nerves are needed in order to accurately grasp information and respond to changes in timely manner.

NINJUTSU—THE ART OF THE NINJA

Another important point that Mr. Ohno constantly made to companies was, "It is quick, flexible operations that managers need, not mathematical operations."

Mathematical operations manage a company based on mathematical calculations, often performed in offices far from the actual manufacturing floor. In other words, they are simple operations that calculate profit by subtracting necessary costs from sales. Anyone with rational thinking and calculation skills can do it. Ninjutsu operations, on the other hand, require high level skills that can only be learned through training.

Ninjutsu, the art of the Ninja, is something that can be learned through strict training. The Ninjutsu art of jumping over high walls, water-escapes, and fire-escapes, are attainable only through many years of hard training. In my view, there are too many managers today who forget about training, but because they are good at mathematics they try to figure everything out by numbers.

In other words, there are too many managers who operate like the proverb "not seeing the forest for the trees."

What managers need to do is grow the forest instead of growing a single tree; Maximize employees' ingenuity, gather them, and transform them into the energy needed for the company to grow. Managers need to understand the mathematics, but more importantly they need to educate people who are skilled and unique. Education and training to maximize the potential skills of people should be the most important focus for managers, who need to view the long-term perspective, not the pursuit of immediate profit while making light of training and education.

Managers do not deserve their position and title when they are absorbed in balancing the books instead of working with their employees, because they place excessive importance on pleasing stock holders. True managers are those who confidently work to educate people in spite of any criticism they may face. Companies who are led by such managers will win the long-term race, in spite of any disadvantages in the short-term.

How TPS Training Influenced Stock Prices

Stock Values

Company Name		1980	1981	1982	1983	1984	1985	1986	1987	1988	1989	1990	1991	1992	1993	1994	1995	1996	1997	1998	1999	2000
Asics	max.	480	634	595	570	539	450	683	668	784	1040	1020	662	535	580	513	397	426	276	157	175	138
	min.	343	403	458	458	365	355	400	450	502	706	411	440	316	355	360	228	260	80	60	90	96
Tostem	max.						4800	3610	3280	2315											2620	1931
	min.						2900	3060	1110	1100											1731	1300
Aichi Electric	max.	215	186	170	230	424	498	789	746	755	1690	2470	2130	1340	1300	965	740	669	555	359	236	260
	min.	178	159	118	130	185	290	365	550	530	650	930	1190	560	620	690	352	500	185	210	170	185
KOA	max.	394	565	478	899	1330	960	800	720	960	1090	1350	942	952	820	1810	1770	1820	2070	1465	3150	3750
	min.	240	355	270	310	820	529	405	381	550	730	650	580	406		1220	970	1320	790	790	853	1800
Mitsumi Electric	max.	626	506	443	1080	1530	1330	1420	1450	1270	1270	2400	1890	1260	2020	2230	2630	2580	3390	2845	3970	4650
	min.	415	370	285	371	760	625	810	790	885	920	1000	1040	668	1060	1230	1260	1520	1770	1750	1838	1785
Sony	max.	3550	5860	4460	3910	4270	5040	4190	5710	7290	9500	9150	7180	4530	5570	6460	6230	7700	12600	13490	30300	33900
	min.	1510	3010	2830	3050	3170	3310	2800	2560	4600	6550	5360	3980	3350	3850	5000	3730	6040	7250	7230	7290	23430
NEC	max.	602	933	991	1560	1550	1370	2490	2640	2390	2060	2290	1710	1250	1060	1310	1520	1430	1750	1560	2665	3450
	min.	362	530	662	880	1020	900	1140	1310	1680	1690	1220	1100	606	601	859	653	1060	1240	762	1012	1899
Nippon Chemi-Con	max.	795	975	720	1090	1440	1260	1120	1430	1590	1360	1400	1230	878	771	778	770	777	707	620	571	948
	min.	518	645	441	490	830	651	760	720	939	1070	710	610	381	449	526	403	511	277	293	314	355
Rohm	max.				9840	14500	8100	5130	6520	5500	4490	5830	3300	2880	3410	4680	6750	7680	15600	16050	44000	42200
	min.				6720	4440	2780	2530	2090	2950	2940	1960	1980	1590	1800	3230	3030	5550	7130	8920	9900	20000
Hirose Electric	max.	1490	2490	1970	4350	6350	4020	3960	5660	6020	6020	7550	3600	3950	6150	6830	6950	7040	9850	8490	23560	23710
	min.	1000	1390	1250	1500	2990	1690	2720	2090	3250	3580	4800	3290	2810	3680	5650	4650	5550	5700	5700	7500	10410
Stanley Electric	max.	524	554	465	837	1180	1100	989	1120	1450	1450	1280	1030	760	824	852	755	631	680	518	745	1357
	min.	387	373	320	425	560	680	715	563	875	992	652	600	471	521	616	520	631	320	312	324	496
Clarion	max.	969	955	911	1240	900	829	682	985	1420	1180	1240	1650	1360	670	618	541	683	590	610	967	970
	min.	735	580	539	752	558	521	453	440	741	832	540	550	337	295	410	310	426	305	275	300	251
Canon	max.	930	1910	1300	1800	1690	1500	1220	1410	1690	2040	1960	1660	1470	1560	1820	1940	2630	3820	3400	4200	5620
	min.	570	785	638	1050	1050	880	870	682	905	1360	1360	1200	1200	1270	1530	1230	1780	2280	1930	2170	3400
Osaki Electric	max.	345	440	296	425	748	799	1400	1430	1630	1750	1810	1540	1120	1090	1080	840	948	718	525	630	850
	min.	246	220	220	230	355	500	730	750	1010	1250	929	990	460	581	745	487	576	242	261	310	425
Tokin	max.	527	708	618	1260	1040	1350	1730	1470	1500	2910	1070	1020	1240	1240	1710	1710	1010	1710	1050	958	1635
	min.	346	370	442	507						1600						860		670	485	500	536

▨ In Progress

Figure 7: How TPS Training Influenced Company Stock Prices

Managers should focus on training their employees because they are the people who will sustain and grow the organization in the long run. Employees are the future of a company.

Yamada's Lean Lesson No. 18

"Solid production management is as important as the contractor's plans for building a house. Operations must be adjusted accordingly for everything to be completed together, and in the proper order.

If there is no skill in the operations, we call it "Sechin Daiku" (an unskilled carpenter)."

TRUST WORKERS AND YOU WON'T NEED TO MANAGE THEM

The 20th Century saw the realization of mass production and the progress of scientific management techniques. The scientific management technique of scheduling involves the analysis and standardization of every task a factory worker performs. This is compiled and sent to a planning department where they, away from the manufacturing floor, draw a work schedule based upon the analysis and standards. Workers perform their own tasks according to the predetermined work standard and schedule, and one supervisor is assigned to one functional division to control the workers. Employees who work above and beyond the standard get compensated more than those who work less.

This was the first scientific control method and system of efficiency. The system later became the standard scholastic and operations theory used in the U.S.

I believe that the operations theory of the 20th Century is a complete failure in the sense of maximizing and nurturing each individual's skills and promoting each person's fresh ideas to create improvements. Ideally, there should be no need for managers because people should be trained to think for themselves and problem solve on their own. Because we have become so accustomed to outsourcing our work to the cheapest available source, however, it becomes difficult for management to see the value in properly training their workforce. Companies continue to outsource their work because they do not recognize the innate talents of their employees.

More U.S. companies in recent years are shifting to the paradigm of prioritizing their customers and stockholders, instead of focusing on internal improvement. Is this really good? A company's existence is supported by its employees. Employees' quality determines the performance of a company because the employees are the people who actually serve the company's customers. Treat employees well and continue nurturing them and it will naturally lead to sound operations.

PRODUCTION FLOOR THAT BECAME A BLACK BOX

Where does money come from in the manufacturing industry? Some people might say it comes from a specific department, such as Research & Development. I can say, however, without a doubt that it is the production floor that produces the money. This worries me, however, because it appears that the people who look at the production floor have lost their ability to truly *see* the production floor.

Consultants, managers, supervisors of a production department, and even factory managers have lost the eyes to look at factories. What I mean by having the 'eyes to look at factories' is the ability to see, seek out, and acknowledge wasteful activities and the harm that such activities can create for the company.

Companies today, unlike decades past, produce value-added products that are sold not only domestically but overseas as well. What makes the production of value-added products possible is the tremendous effort taken to create good products, the perseverance to continue test after test, and the creative ideas to make better products based on the Genchi Gembutsu (Go and See) theory. Everyone once understood how to actually read a factory. The reason value-added products are no longer manufactured is that we have lost the ability to truly read a factory. As a result, the manufacturing industry as a whole is in a critical situation.

How have we lost the ability to read a factory? It is because information has become less accessible and more confusing; and computerized controls account for much of this. Computers control many things, such as the automatic ordering of materials, and these tasks are often performed from a control room far away from a production floor. The people in charge of these tasks can even get by without ever setting foot on a production floor. The people who believe this is the most rational way of working most often have a bias toward computers being the most ideal way of doing business. The truth is that very important things are lost if production is controlled in such a way. If you use your own hands to produce items, the sense of accomplishment you receive leads to confidence and pride in your work.

Some people even go so far as to say that unmanned factories would be the ultimate accomplishment. However, if factories are completely unmanned there will no longer be *any* eyes to see the factory. We must not turn a factory into a black box. It is true that machines make things, but it is humans that set the machines up to make value-added products through many trials and the testing of their ideas. Factories and manufacturing floors are the most interesting and revealing laboratories. It is humans with the eyes to see a manufacturing floor who can play the main role in improving the manufacturing industry.

Yamada's Lean Lesson No. 19

"Manufacturers must regain the ability to read a factory. If you lose this ability to read a plant, you will not get a second chance to stand on your own two feet again. Without the ability to read a factory, the opportunity to recover is lost forever."

EVALUATE SKILL DIFFERENCES ACCURATELY

No two products on the market today are the same, in spite of the fact that most products are standardized. This is due to the difference in the skills between the many different manufacturers. The skill differences should be identified accurately in order to reflect the prices of their products. To give an example of price differences based upon skill differences: The price of paintings are much different among different artists, and even if paintings are created by the same artist the prices vary depending upon appraisals and the motifs of the paintings. Similarly, now is the time for the industrial society to evaluate the market, otherwise manufacturing will continue endlessly toward price reduction.

It is our most urgent assignment to regain manufacturing strength by building a system that respects skilled workers and recognizes their differences in skills and techniques. As soon as you stop treating all employees the same and begin recognizing their various styles and quality of work, both employee engagement and product quality will improve.

Most management personnel believe that the reason for the hardships the manufacturing industry is facing today is slow sales. It is understandably difficult to increase sales in a slow economy, however, this does not mean management needs to constantly cry out for cost reduction and increased sales. Management is not needed at all if simply shouting out what everyone already knows could solve problems. What management needs to do is not expand their companies but create a workplace where employees can grow personally and professionally while enjoying their work on manufacturing floors. Build the ideal manufacturing environment where every worker finds joy in working and works hard to discover their own skills and working techniques. It is then the job of managers to clearly identify employees skills and qualities to build a company wide evaluation process that reveals the training needs of each worker.

Company Complacency Prevents Individual Growth

When I define a typical large corporation, this is what I see:

- A company where many employees do the same work
- A company where many employees do not produce added value
- A company where many employees consider facilities, appearances, and titles important
- A company where you can survive without mingling with outside people
- A company which can procure cheap loans from a bank

Generally speaking, many large companies have a culture where standards are prioritized above all else and employees repeat the same work day after day. If you work for such a company, any skills outside those you employ to perform your repeated daily tasks will degrade more and more with each passing day. This is because large companies often employ the Division of Labor System. A task that one person can do is deliberately divided to make it more complicated. Because of this division, a task that could normally be done without problem can become extremely difficult to do. When you suggest a new challenge, your suggestion is denied because there is no model for them to follow.

When I visit a large company and notice employees who seem to have lost their passion and the will to do their work, I give them a warning, "You graduated from good colleges and I believe you must have been excellent employees when you first started working at the company. But if you continue as you are now, no one will hire you once you are finished with this job." Then I add, "Do you have skills that can be used at other companies too? If you think about your workplace as a school without tuition and try every day to learn various new skills, I am sure that other companies will come to hire you without you seeking them out."

Often, however, they do not listen to my warnings earnestly. Their unhappiness started from finding employment at a large company, where their daily joy in work was slowly stifled to nothingness. Please review the large company images that I mentioned before. If your company sounds like what is mentioned there, now is the time to make a change.

BECOME A DILIGENT CITIZEN

Every citizen must become diligent in order to save their country from facing extreme hardships. There is no way to save a country when it is facing a life or death situation if its citizens do not take their work seriously. People around the world would hesitate extending their support to the failing country, believing that it is the country's own fault for the peril they are in. Citizens must turn over a new leaf and become diligent, as they once were, and strive to be the best model in the world. In today's world, the word "diligent" itself has almost become a dead word. When it becomes a dead word completely, the world will be in a perpetual state of crisis. We must all unite and tackle the difficulties that we face together in order to bring about lasting positive change.

When I say "diligent," I do not mean to work long hours; I mean "to be a good worker." You do not want to give up your ingenuity to do meaningful work. A road will open up for you when everyone does meaningful work.

The great Spanish writer Cervantes says in his book "Don Quixote":
"Diligence is the mother of happiness."

Yamada's Lean Lesson No. 20

"People who do not question how they perform their work can never eliminate Muda.
The starting point for identifying and eliminating waste is to question how work is performed."

Photo 6: Business Professionals in Tokyo

4

なぜあなたにはムダが見えないのか？

WHY IS MUDA INVISIBLE TO YOU?

REMOVING MUDA IS PART OF YOUR JOB, NOT EXTRA WORK

How do you define Muda in your own life? This idea is difficult to define and even Mr. Ohno was at a loss for a moment when he was asked, "What is Muda?"

"Muda is to get no rewards," said Mr. Ohno, and he continued, "When you go for an errand for someone and you get no rewards, you call it Muda. Nobody wants to go for an errand if they receive no reward in return."

Most people don't understand or work to eliminate waste because they don't see any reward for them to do so — no acknowledgement of the removal of waste. What people need to understand, however, is that the removal of Muda benefits them by creating a better quality of life. To me, the definition of Muda as it relates to a person is "selectively spending money that will add value to the goods or service you are paying for."

To explain this further, let's take an example of a typical activity that most people encounter: shopping. Whether shopping for clothing, food, or other items, it has become commonplace to have miscellaneous items placed just before or along the checkout lines. These items are placed there to entice you to purchase them impulsively; making it easy to not think through a purchase. However, if you did not plan to go to the store to purchase a magazine or candy bar, the purchase holds no meaning and is more often than not a cause for regret afterward. This is nothing but a waste. There is no value added to your shopping experience if you came in to purchase groceries for the week and left with a magazine that looked interesting but that holds no great importance to your life.

However, if you went in search of a magazine to read and found what you were looking for in line at the checkout counter at the store, this would be a value added purchase. There would be more satisfaction in finding the item that you were seeking out and in selectively spending your money in a manner that benefits you. The difference between these two ways of purchasing (impulse vs. planned) is intent and purpose.

Unconscious Motion Is Waste

In order to manufacture goods, a series of pro-cesses must flow smoothly from raw materials, to assembly, and finally to finished goods. If a delay occurs, it is because there is waste in the process. What causes waste then? As the title of this section suggests, unconscious motion can be seen as waste.

For example, unintentional motions such as look-ing back or reaching to grab parts cause waste. You need to limit your motions as much as possible to eliminate waste. Waste reduction at a factory starts from this idea. At first people will be doubtful it can be done, however once waste reduction practice starts people will begin to see its positive effects.

Once people clearly understand that their efforts are paid off, they actively begin to identify wasteful motions; no one wants to be doing things that are wasteful. Furthermore, people begin to ask them-selves, "Is there anything else here that is waste?" and they begin to see waste removal as an enjoyable practice. As more people become aware of waste and start thinking up their own small ideas to eliminate waste, their individual efforts will become a com-pany-wide effort. Once they reach this point, waste elimination efforts will progress dramatically.

Lean, or the practice of Muda-tori, is not limited to manufacturing floors alone, though. The same thing can be used in an office or retail environment. Think critically about what you do each day to find out if your motions are creating waste or not. You will begin to see waste in your motions if you truly make an effort to dissect what motions you go through each day.

> ### *Yamada's Lean Lesson No. 21*
>
> *"Develop a strong desire to carry out what you have learned.*
> *It is more important to apply your knowledge to your work than to simply learn."*

DETAILED OPERATION PLANNING LEADS TO MUDA-TORI

If you must manufacture a certain volume of products in an hour, how do you determine how much material and how many processes are needed, how do you assign different tasks, and to whom? This task falls to the person in charge of production control, who mathematically determines the day's production schedule based upon information he/she has received. They then summarize this information into a plan in order to share the plan with everyone else on the shop floor.

Making such a plan is very common at manufacturing facilities, but is not often seen in office environments. This is because there has never been a dedicated person who is in charge of the daily operations of an office. To understand this point better, choose an administrative worker and ask them to summarize the operational plan on a given day for their department. Nobody will be able to summarize such a report, not even a department manager. Managers *should* be preparing such a plan, but unlike production management of a factory they have a difficult time calculating objectives, numbers, and targets.

A plan of the general office is often very vague and does not show clearly by whom and by what time jobs need to be completed. Managers assign certain tasks to each person based upon their job title, hoping nothing disastrous will happen and each day will turn out the same as yesterday. This is nothing but the accumulation of waste from each day tumbling into the next. People do not even notice what they are doing is waste. From my view point, there are many cases in which people spend all day on work that can be normally done in one hour. I believe that if white-collar workers make concrete business plans each day and ensure their plans are known to everyone, just like production control managers do, they can eliminate waste and increase their productivity.

Your Work Transforms Itself Through Productivity Improvement

After graduating from college I worked as a newspaper reporter. My work was to write one article a day, due by midnight. After a year or so I was able to finish my work in just 40 or 50 minutes, in addition to becoming very proficient at finding news. Because I had streamlined my process there was no longer a need for me to get worked up over every deadline. When I went out for lunch I played Han-Chan Mahjong. I returned to my office around 4 o'clock and started writing again. Even so, I was able to easily finish my job by the deadline.

If my life as a newspaper reporter continued along in that manner I wouldn't be where I am today. Fortunately, when I was 26 years old I noticed how complacent and unproductive I had become, being at work for 8 hours and only needing 1 hour to complete my time, so I began looking for a job where I could be more productive. My monthly salary at that time was about 20,000 Yen ($200) but an acquaintance of mine, who was a management consultant, was making over 20,000 Yen for only 2 hours of work.

> "If there is a job for me where I can make money like that, I'd quit my job as a newspaper reporter," I thought.

I am the kind of person who sets his/her ideas in action immediately. I started studying to become a consultant at a production department right away, but of course there was no quick way that I could start working. My idea to get started right away, then, was to organize a seminar with my acquaintance. If a lot of people turned up, we could begin to make a profit. Otherwise, we would end up in the red. Fortunately for us, we had many participants in the seminar, most likely because a seminar was still a new approach in those days. I was making the most money I ever had just by holding seminars 4 days a month.

By becoming more productive at my newspaper job I didn't have to spend as much time working and that gave me enough spare time to pursue other activities, which made me what I am today. That proves that your work could easily transform if you think about improving the productivity of your work, no matter what kind of work it is. The important thing to focus on is finding anything that may be wasting your time as quickly as possible so that you can begin to eliminate it. The trick is to discover a way to be more productive, whether by finding someone else to help you or by analyzing your own work to find how you can remove wastes. Step out of your comfort zone and critically view the way you are currently working so that you can improve yourself and be more productive.

Yamada's Lean Lesson No. 22

"Business professionals must have an understanding of a work schedule, on a daily basis, to understand what work needs to be completed in what amount of time.
The most important thing is to constantly be looking for ways to reduce lead times and make their work as efficient as possible."

BEWARE LOSING YOUR SENSE OF TIME

Business professionals in particular must be aware of wasting their time. When you repeat the same work day after day it is difficult to notice how wastefully you spend your time. This is because it becomes easy to lose your sense of time. Most people believe that tomorrow and the day after tomorrow will be there, just like today. That is why you postpone your work, thinking that you can do it tomorrow. That is no good. We must all constantly work under the assumption that there is no tomorrow. If you think that you have just today left to complete your work, you would not leave work half finished.

For example, let's imagine that you must write and submit a report. If you postpone it thinking that you can do it tomorrow, your work could take 3 or 4 months. On the other hand, if you focus on writing a portion of your report each day, you would be able to easily finish the report within 1 month. You can set up your target date even more precisely by dividing your schedule into smaller segments; for example, finishing 10 pages of the report between 1 o'clock and 3 o'clock.

A business professional, as it is defined, is thought to be extremely efficient and is therefore busy every day. Business professionals, as the word implies, are considered to be busy people. In reality, however, they do not actually plan or schedule specific work times, so they are simply doing work as they find it, which is a waste. It seems to me that business professionals have lost their sense of time and they just appear to be working busily all the time.

Make A Daily Action Plan Before You Go to Work

When you have a sense of time, you can plan your time well. The people I have met who plan and control their day's schedule are very competent business professionals. However, if they are striving to become a truly superior business professional, they will not simply stop there. Once they make their day's schedule, the next thing that they need to do is to make an hourly schedule. They must make their action plans and try to act according to their schedule as much as possible. Unfortunately, I rarely see business people who plan on an hour by hour basis.

For most people, making a general daily schedule is the most they can do and very few people are actually able to follow their daily schedules well. A majority of business professionals go to work without thinking anything at all. It is only once they sit at their desks that they begin to think about their day's work. Thus, they cannot accomplish anything substantial before around 10 o'clock in the morning. They waste at least a whole hour during the most productive time of day deciding what it is they much accomplish that day. It is a loss for a company and above all it is a huge waste of the business professional's time that cannot be returned. Even so, their superiors are not aware of this fact and there is no one who is able to point it out to them. If proper training is given, however, I believe that employees can start working at full speed upon their arrival at work.

In the long run, their efforts will blossom as a significant improvement in their capabilities.

Yamada's Lean Lesson No. 23

"To say "I cannot do it" means to say you are not skilled enough to do it.

To say "It is difficult for me" means to say that you aren't willing to change the way you work, to be flexible enough to react to changing environments."

APPLY THE CYCLE TIME CONCEPT TO OFFICE OPERATIONS

The Toyota Production System, focused upon total elimination of waste, invented the concept of "Cycle Time". Mr. Ohno differentiated the concept of Cycle Time from that of Takt Time, in order to respond to Actual Customer Orders at any given moment. I have chosen to use the concept of Cycle Time in this chapter because of my strong desire to preserve Mr. Ohno's philosophy that the most effective way to manage a business is to balance daily production volume by producing to meet customers' actual daily orders, not by over producing based on historical data (Takt Time) or future forecasts to achieve Just-in-Time.

What Mr. Ohno communicated, and I support, is that we need to get the Actual Customer Order information from the office down to the shop floor. To do this we first need to truly understand the difference between Takt Time and Cycle Time. *(See Figure 8)* To illustrate this point we will look at businesses operations as they typically stand today, utilizing Takt Time, and then the more advanced methods of using Cycle Time to plan each day in a manufacturing setting.

Figure 8: Understanding the Difference Between Takt Time and Cycle Time

Takt Time is defined as available time divided by average customer demand. But the concept was developed during the mass production era in Japan and was measured in months or years, not hours or minutes. The Takt Time concept looked at historical data and future projections because if Toyota produced more, more cars could be sold. This is not true today, so more emphasis needs to be placed on Cycle Time, as we are not able to accurately produce to customer demand based upon general aggregate Takt Time forecasting. Today we have multi-mix low-volume production—many types of products at relatively low volumes. In this reality we need measurements that are not aggregated, but specific to actual sellable products in order to build products precisely to daily customer orders.

To do this we need to calculate the Cycle Time

for each specific product in the factory and have the ability to use this information on an hourly basis throughout the day. We still need to look at some historical information, but we must only use this data to calculate the resource plan for production, not to manage production. Takt Time should only be used to determine how the use of raw materials and resources is projected to be used during the up-coming month. To further clarify:

First Step: Calculate Takt Time

1. Estimate the amount of sales for a month based on past sales records (3 months).

2. Estimate the planned production volume for one day. This is found by dividing the production volume for one month (actual historical customer orders) by the number of working days in the month with accomodations for known demand fluxuations.

Second Step: Actual Product(s) Cycle Times

3. Determine the Cycle Time by dividing the daily working hours by the daily volume of orders to be shipped (actual received customer orders).

People in charge of sales and production first calculate the average volume of sales from the past 3 months of actual sales and adjust the average sales by various other factors, such as seasonality, current sales trends, and so on. This is used not to produce products at Takt Time but to plan the capacity needs of the business and ensure there are enough resources and materials to support such volumes. *(See Figure 8)* This calculated value becomes the planning volume for the month. We must make use of the aspects of the old production system that are still useful, and that is setting up the capabilities of the operation to have the resources necessary to produce Actual Customer Orders at varying daily demand rates. Again, I must stress that the most important thing here is to use Takt Time to plan production, not to produce; Takt Time ensures you have the appropriate raw materials and resources to produce to Actual Daily Orders.

To go back to the Cycle Time concept:

New Way: Actual Product Cycle Times

- Actual Product Cycle Time is the time determined by dividing the daily working hours by actual customer orders to be shipped.

This calculation is used by the line, cell, or area supervisor in the morning and updated every hour, as more orders are received during the day. They receive the actual customer orders from sales and immediately calculate each product's Cycle Time for the day. The mix and volume numbers will be different every time, so the Takt Time concept of averaging production is not useful as it will make some production run slower and some faster. This is muda. When you are not producing to stock you need defined measurements for each specific product. This is the power of the Cycle Time concept. It allows workers to plan their own production, mix labor where needed, delay on some production until later in the day, change production on an hourly basis, self-manage their daily demands while still making the delivery schedule, and have time for Kaizen. No other measurement can provide this level of empowerment to each worker.

As far as the shop floor is concerned, always following the concept of Cycle Time is a fundamental requirement to sustaining Muda-tori on a daily basis. As managers you will need to educate your staff, help them develop production control boards, and bring the concept of Cycle Time to your shop floor through the use of various communication and documentation tools—this is not easy but is necessary for today's reality to match daily customer orders. Each worker must be aware of this. If work can be done faster than a Cycle Time, it means the work itself has leeway and the worker has time to assist on another line, cell, or process. If work cannot be done within a given Cycle Time, each worker must signal for help and assistance.

The greatest advantage to applying the concept of Cycle Time is that it allows each worker to take a leadership role in adjusting his/her own production cycles based on actual production progress at any given time. After putting each worker in charge of his/her own production, by the use of Cycle Time

Concept, I have witnessed many workers who have raised their awareness toward Kaizen and proactively implemented ideas to achieve dramatic increases in work efficiency, often over 30%.

This concept should also be brought to the office, to help business people plan their daily, weekly, and monthly work. Calculating Cycle Times for all recurring work will allow a person to schedule other projects, plans, and commitments without over-stressing their week. By understanding the Cycle Time of their work, each person has the ability to flexibly adjust their schedule and create a daily working plan. Successful businesses have seen 50% increase in office efficiency when implementing the Cycle Time Concept.

Workers ought not to be treated like machines. Their motivation comes from the ability to control their own environment. This greatly affects morale and engagement toward work on a daily basis.

SPENDING TOO MUCH TIME IN MEETINGS IS WASTEFUL

Most business professionals constantly say, "I'm too busy." However, they do not appear to notice how wastefully they are spending their time. When I call managers or executives to schedule a time to meet, our conversation always seems to follow the same pattern.

"Do you have some time available today?"

"I'm sorry but I have a meeting today."

They say they have meetings on this day and that day, so they do not even have the time to talk over the phone. They sound like they are in meetings all the time. On the other hand, when they have no meetings, on rare occasions, their reply is, "Please come in." In other words, what they truly mean is, "Please come anytime when we have no meetings scheduled."

It appears that the job of managers and executives is to attend meetings and they have determined their other jobs are less important than the meetings. I am grateful that they recognize that my consultations are useful to them, however, looking from a different perspective it means that managers and executives are doing nothing more worthwhile than sitting in meetings. Nothing is more wasteful than a meeting that drags on and on with no purpose. If the purpose of a meeting is simply to make something known to everyone, emails can easily accomplish that task. Everyone can check their emails at a convenient time in order to save time. It is wrong to use meetings as an excuse to not work. It is my opinion that companies should work hard to reduce meetings so that people cannot use the excuse "I do not have time because I have a meeting to attend."

I believe that communication with people outside of their companies is much more valuable than wasting their time in non-lucrative internal meetings.

> ### *Yamada's Lean Lesson No. 24*
>
> "Our lives consist of roughly 30,000 days.
> If your goal is to maximize your time then
> you can never allow yourself to ignore
> wasteful work.
> Life is too short to be wasteful."

AIM FOR BETTER QUALITY WORK AND A 100% SUCCESS RATE

Because business professionals are paid on a salary basis, their pay does not change no matter how busy they are in a month. This is a big problem. Business professionals will become more sensitive about how they work and spend their time if there is a system that pays people on a daily basis instead of monthly and according to the contributions they make each day. If they must come up with concrete results each day, no one would spend their time idly.

In the monthly and annual pay system, people do not need to think very hard about how they should spend their time. In the annual pay system, many people pretend they are working hard only when the time for salary review approaches, thinking "It's around that time again, I should flatter my boss a little."

The annual pay system can work for other organizations, such as sports, but it does not belong in the business world. The reason the annual pay system for professional baseball players works is that it is easy to evaluate each player's performance accurately, thereby they are able to base pay off of the information gathered each year. For example, computing how many positive points to give for one home run and negative points for strikeout, etc. In that respect, it is difficult to evaluate business professional's performances accurately. Performance evaluations for people in charge of marketing is a little bit easier, as the results of their efforts are shown in real numbers, however it is difficult to evaluate the results of a regular desk job.

There are many business professionals fooling themselves, believing that they are working if they just sit at their desks doing only what they are told. That is wasteful to begin with. I think the fastest way to eliminate waste from a business professional's workplace is to change the annual and monthly pay system to the daily allowance, whereby each person will become more sensitive to the quality and density of their daily work.

Six Hours of Your Working Day Are Waste

The length of time that humans can really concentrate on the same subject or project is about 2 hours, at most. For example, 1 hour is the concentration limit for a boxing match, 2 hours for a baseball game, and a little less than 2 hours for a soccer game with a break in the middle. 2 hours would be the concentration limit for practicing piano. People can actually concentrate on what they are doing on a single task or project only that long without a break out of 24 hours a day.

In spite of that, working hours are usually set at 8 hours a day. However, it is not feasible, not truly possible, for people to continuously concentrate on what they are doing for 8 solid hours. Whatever work you are doing, 2 hours is the limit that you can really concentrate. That means that people are wasting 6 hours of their working day. Unfortunately, there are very few business professionals who truly take notice of this. They dawdle along 8 hours a day because their working hours are set at 8 hours. Conversely, 8 hours a day means you will spread your work out over 8 hours, even if you can do the same work in just 2 hours. If that is the case, we are better off eliminating the working hours in a day, thus people can make good use of their remaining time on something else.

While business professionals continue to work in this way, people in the developing countries are working hard to strengthen their power more and more each day. There is no place in the fiercely competitive business world for humans who intently strive to make their lives easier without noticing all the waste that they are creating.

In the software development industry, people in India have already committed to being the best in the world. It is only a matter of the time before Japan is surpassed by China in the manufacturing industry, in which people believed Japan would always be on top. Now is the time for everyone to realize just how much time we are wasting. If we do not notice and eliminate waste we will be left behind by the rest of the world. I believe that without a sense of impending crisis, we will be unable to eliminate waste no matter how much time passes.

It Is Too Late to Notice Waste Just Before Your Retirement

Japanese business professionals do not notice that they are running on the road of ruin. They are satisfied with their career advancement from a subsection chief, a section chief, to a department head, and so on. They do not believe that they are really running on the road of ruin. When most business professionals retire, at the age of 60, that is when they truly take notice of how wastefully they have spent their time. They are at a loss when their job titles are gone from their business cards and they notice that they have no marketable skills and competencies that they can be proud of. There is still time left to change and some hope left for older generations who are fortunate enough to receive ample retirement allowances.

However, we are now in the era when there are no such guarantees even at large companies, as organizational reform and large-scale restructuring are taking place. People without any marketable skills or confidence are in turmoil after their retirement, thinking, "I'm in trouble! I want to work but I cannot find anyone who will hire me."

90% of business professionals who are approaching their retirement only notice that they are in a serious situation approximately 6 months before their retirement. I am often asked, "Sir, do you know anyone who can hire me?" It is too late at that point to ask me a favor like that. Honestly, there is no way to help them because they have been too caught up in their daily work and have not noticed at all that they have been wasting their time for so long. If they notice Muda at an earlier stage and try to apply Muda-tori each day, after about 3 years they can achieve something that they never imagined before. The important thing is at which point in time they begin to notice Muda. That time is the turning point to whether or not their second life, after retirement, is fulfilled.

I believe that people who laugh at Muda-tori may come to grief after their retirement. People who have seriously tackled Muda-tori are the people who can enjoy their victory and laugh at the end.

Yamada's Lean Lesson No. 25

"90% of a business professional's work is repetitive (checking emails, etc.); and as long as something has a pattern/sequence, you can manage it.

Once you manage your work by time and volume, your value-added work becomes clear to you.

Quality & volume become clear to you if you manage this pattern."

You Can Eliminate Waste by Changing Your Management Style

Companies are not good at labor management and tend to let their workers do wasteful things. For instance, most companies subcontract a cleaning company to take care of their cleaning needs and employees of a cleaning company are paid on an hourly basis. No employees would think about doing their work efficiently when they are paid by the hour because if they work efficiently their actual working hours are shortened and, as a result, they get paid less.

It is understandable that no one wants to do things that may reduce his/her pay. So what should be done to increase their efficiency then? One way is to stop the hourly pay system and establish a pay system that is based on individual work assignment. Each employee is assigned certain rooms to clean and he/she can go home after finishing his/her assignment. If any employees want more rooms to clean, they would try to increase their efficiency and competitiveness to achieve greater productivity, thereby increasing their available earnings.

Along those same lines of wasteful management, in my view hotels have one of the most wasteful working environments, right behind factories. It seems to me hotels are made up of bundles, or pockets, of waste. Several hotel service persons are involved between a person's arrival at a hotel and the time they finally get to their room. This is a hallmark of the Division of Labor System. Most of the time, one customer is served by several hotel employees, depending on the type of service the customer is seeking (concierge, valet parking, room service, etc.). I believe waste can be eliminated if the workflow of a hotel is reformed in such a way that one hotel employee is assigned to one room and takes care of everything for their customer, from check in through check out.

Some customers may prefer being served by several hotel employees but many people, like myself, feel that it is a nuisance to be served by different people. Hotel customers would have greater peace of mind if one person was assigned to take care of them, instead of changing service persons for different services. The employees would also then have more opportunities to use their own ideas to do their jobs better and thus feel more satisfaction in their work. Of course, this way of operating would make the process more efficient from a managerial perspective as well.

I would like to suggest that you go to a hotel and observe the behaviors and services of the employees. It will open your eyes to what waste is all about.

BECOME LEAN TO OUTPERFORM YOUR COMPETITORS

Managers and business professionals lay the blame on the economy for their poor business and it is common these days to hear, "Our business is poor because the economy is sluggish." However, this way of thinking is a big mistake. I dare to say that poor business and a slow economy often have nothing to do each other. The reason for a company's poor business is a lack of a skilled workforce, with business executives at the head of the list. You can sell good products even in a slow economy. As a matter of fact, there are some companies that actually increase their sales during a sluggish economy.

For example, Fujix, one of the companies of Fuji Films Group, has quadrupled its sales in 4 years as a result of the breakthrough development of digital cameras. Among the larger companies, Honda has developed the popular small car Fit and its domestic and overseas sales jumped to second in sales, just behind Toyota.

The reason why people moan about poor sales is that they treat everything in an equal and egalitarian manner. That is why they say, "Our business is poor because other companies' business is poor." If a company has one thing that is superior to any other company's, it can easily say "We are doing just fine even when business for other companies are poor."

As a simple example, we need people like the baseball player Ichiro Suzuki to get out of this paradigm. For Ichiro, it didn't matter whether his team, Orix, could win or not, or that the popularity of Japanese baseball is declining. This didn't matter because he was capable of becoming, and has become, a baseball star on his own in the U.S. If a company has three outstanding persons like him it could certainly survive through a turbulent economy no matter how severe it becomes.

Some of the readers may object, saying that it is difficult to gather people like Ichiro. However, we never know where superior talents are. I hear that even Ichiro was playing for the farm team at first and his talent was not recognized at all in those days. If you think that your employees are all only ordinary people, provide them with the means to tackle their workplace efficiency creatively. Their talents will certainly come alive once they are awakened by waste elimination practices.

It is easier than you think to get out of the paradigm of treating everything in an equal and egalitarian manner once each employee begins to put forth an effort to eliminate Muda thoroughly. What is needed to change the profitability of your business is a focus on Muda-tori practices and the elimination of waste. Once you change your perspective you will no longer treat everything and everyone in an equal and egalitarian manner.

Yamada's Lean Lesson No. 26

"Ask your workforce if they have accomplished their task, and not if they understand the principle.
Management is not effective if you only understand and never take action to implement the principles learned."

WORK IS WHERE YOU USE YOUR WISDOM AND IDEAS

Mr.Taiichi Ohno told me a story of when he gave a lecture in Taiwan. Mr. Ohno often spoke about the difference between the two words "move" and "work," so of course he talked about it in Taiwan too. His lecture was running along smoothly, drawing the audiences' attention, when suddenly the interpreter interrupted him.

"I am sorry but there is no such word as "work" with the person character in Chinese."

Mr. Ohno did not understand what he meant at first. He thought it was strange that there was no such a word as "work" in China, the country where Chinese characters originated from. But the interpreter looked serious and soon Mr. Ohno realized that the interpreter was not joking. The lecture ended well but Mr. Ohno was still concerned about what the interpreter meant by there being no such character as "work" in Chinese. After he returned home he checked in a dictionary to find that the Chinese character "work" was actually created in Japan.

The word "work" does not just mean to move around. Machines only move; Humans use their brains and wisdom to move with purpose. It becomes work when humans move while eliminating Muda from their movements all the time. We cannot call it work unless you are using your ideas and wisdom.

Figure 9: Japanese Character for "Work" and "Move"

COMPANIES MUST CUSTOMIZE TO SURVIVE

In the manufacturing industry, no manufacturers can succeed by simply selling products at cheap prices. Manufacturers will succeed by creating unique and attractive products through the effort and skill of every employee. Consumers buy products that are attractive and have added value even if their prices are high. The same thing applies to business professionals. Workers will be put on the 'unnecessary manpower' list if they continue to simply be jack of all trades, instead of working to enhance their skills greatly in one area of work. Your presence will become weaker and weaker unless you acquire your own unique skills, although not everyone is born gifted with natural talents. What should we do then?

You only need to check your work closely and drastically eliminate wastes from your work. The important thing is how far you can take it. There are too many business professionals who understand that what they are doing is waste, but they neglect to make any effort to eliminate waste because it is easier for them to simply continue doing things the way they always have. What is waste to you is also waste to your company. Eliminating waste from your work means you are contribution to your company.

Yamada's Lean Lesson No. 27

"Depending on your level of experience in performing Kaizen your point of view will change and allow you to see Muda in a different light.

More Kaizen experience means you will have a greater ability to see waste.

Change how you approach Muda-tori by doing Kaizen."

MUDA BECOMES VISIBLE BY ESTABLISHING STANDARD WORK

It is necessary to have the ability to see waste in order to eliminate it; so how can you learn to identify waste? Simply put, standard work provides the ideal platform to see waste in your work. If you cannot meet your standard it means there is waste somewhere. How much of a difference between your performance and the guidelines of your standard work will tell you how much waste there is.

With well established guidelines, you know how much of your work is wasteful. The way I see it there are very few business professionals who actually follow any standard guidelines, thus they do not see the waste that they create every day. How do we learn to see wastes? I suggest that you create your own standard work, whatever they may look like; however, be wary of guidelines created for you by others because they do not intimately know your work the way you do.

The easiest and the most basic guideline you can make covers the time and volume of your work. The former is to decide how much time you allocate to complete your work. For example, "I'll do this work in one hour" or "I'll do it in two hours." The latter is to decide how much work you want to do in a certain time frame. For example, "I'll do this much work today" or "I'll work on this project in the morning." Refer to your planned schedule constantly while doing your work and create a standard to follow. There are many business professionals who simply going about their work each day, but if they establish their own standards to check their progress I believe that their attitude toward their work will be transformed.

Of course, you must raise the level of your guidelines frequently as your skill levels improve. A goal does not work well unless the level is set at a little higher level than you can easily accomplish; it must be a target you have to stretch to accomplish. Of course, each one of your targets must be relatively small. However, if you achieve each of the small targets completely and continue your effort for 10 or 20 years, your efforts will be more than paid off. Because you have focused on your strengths and stretched yourself to achieve more, you will be unmatched against the business professionals who never did more than they were told.

SET GOALS YOU CAN ACHIEVE 1 OUT OF EVERY 5 ATTEMPTS

I would like to add one more thought regarding how to set up your own standard work. As I mentioned before you should establish your target at a little higher level than you can easily achieve, but how high should it be? If your target is too low, you would not be able to come up with new ideas because work would be too easy. On the other hand, if the target level is too high your enthusiasm and capability would not match up with your target and it would quickly discourage you.

When a coach tells a runner who can run 100 meters in 10 seconds that he could easily run the same distance in 11 seconds the runner will stop practicing. Why should he bother to try harder if he can easily accomplish his goal of winning at a slower pace? There is even a danger that he would get puffed up with pride, which may actually lessen his capabilities.

Conversely, when a coach tells a runner who can run only 100 meters in 12 seconds that he must run the same distance with 10 seconds as his target, it would be a very difficult challenge for the runner. No matter how hard he tries, it would be difficult to achieve that goal. A balance must be struck between accomplishable and not, otherwise the disappointment of the runner will grow and he may lose his confidence. This is the difficult point when establishing your target.

From my experience, a target that you can achieve at the rate of 1 or 2 times out of 5 attempts is the most appropriate level. At this level, you are challenged to hit your target again and again. Needless to say, you must set your target yourself because a target given by someone else is not really a target but a work quota. When you set your own target, you can withstand some pain to achieve your goal. Your satisfaction is greater when you achieve your target, and your accomplishment will be even more satisfying when your target is achievable at the rate of 1 every 5 attempts.

Yamada's Lean Lesson No. 28

"Kaizen is not to simply think about work, but to do it. Perform your task, then review, adjust, and perform the task.
Try it right away & review it—Don't simply plan and think about it."

BE A PERSON WHO RAISES THE AVERAGE

Tokuya Azumi writes a poem called "A Person Who Raises an Average":

> Since that person has come to us
>
> Our workplace has become cheerful
>
> Since that person has come to us
>
> It is a joy to go to work

> Since that person has come to us
>
> Our workplace average has risen so high
>
> A person is great who can raise an average
>
> Every one of us
>
> Be a person who can raise an average

This is one of my favorite poems. What can "an average" be? As an example, at the manufacturing floor of Sanyo Electric that I worked on as a consultant, the most efficient worker can make as many as 45 fax machines in one month by him/herself. On the other hand, the least efficient worker can make only about 25. Now, to make a simple calculation, let's suppose typically a person can make 35 machines, so the average production volume will be set at 35 machines. That means that the workers who can make about 25 machines must make 10 machines more than they usually do.

You may think that the workers would become discouraged and give up, however the workers would instead proactively work to become more efficient, even sometimes give up their break time, and continue working hard. They may sometimes go to more experienced workers for advice. They may feel that it is a burden on the faster workers if the slower workers could not do the work themselves.

An average is only a calculation, however, and it does not mean that everyone must make 35 pieces of the product. Some workers may make more than 35 pieces and other workers may make less than 30. When there is even one worker who challenges the target of 35 pieces, the rest of the workers will naturally try hard to challenge the target too.

Though a target must be established individually, there can also be an average target that everyone can share. Everyone can challenge the same target together because everyone shares it.

Put Yourself in the Right Mindset

I coach many different industries, and what I have found to help people put themselves in the right mindset are:

- Speak clearly and loudly (Be Focused).
- Move briskly (Not Sluggishly).
- Have an objective.

Speaking in a clear and strong voice gives people a cheerful and energetic impression and makes everyone feel good. It makes everyone around you feel excited. On the contrary, a low and weak voice by itself gives the impression of low spirit. Just listening to a low and weak voice disheartens the people around you. It is the same with your movement. Brisk movement gives a healthy impression and motivates people. Unfortunately, people walking sluggishly gives the impression that they have no motivation.

At my company, the PEC Industrial Education Center, we teach people to speak clearly and crisply. It is part of our education program to bring out the confidence and creativity in the employees that are sent to us. We work with people from presidents to managers to shop floor staff, teaching them to become trainers within their own companies. Our Morale Training programs encourage each person to re-discover their inner voice.

Eventually, most people begin to feel joy in saying things clearly and confidently. They transform themselves into positive and confident people, which translates to their work once they have finished their training. Tarzan, the king of the jungle, transforms himself to a wild human by shouting loudly, "Ah! Ah! Ah!" In the same fashion, when you shout loudly and positively, your whole body starts to feel like a new person. Just thinking about speaking loudly and clearly does not work, you must actively participate—which is what we train people to do at PEC.

This is the important point of the work we do. People who complete their training at PEC for a few days return home with a lot of energy, as if they are totally transformed from the person they were when they first showed up. Business professionals too can benefit from this training when they learn to say aloud in strong voice, while facing themselves in a mirror, every morning when they go to work, "Today, I will do it!" This verbal mantra is a very important aspect to changing your way of thinking to a positive mindset.

> ### *Yamada's Lean Lesson No. 29*
>
> "Unless you change your mindset, your actions will not change.
> Work quickly with an energetic voice to change your mindset. This is the starting point to changing your actions."

REMEMBER TO WORK WITH A PURPOSE

I am surprised when I see rush hour scenes in Tokyo, when business people commute during the morning hours rushing up and down the stairs at train stations and disembarking the tightly packed trains with strong purpose. In contrast to the commute, as soon as they arrive at work the energy that made them run up and down the stairs seems to disappear. Their movements suddenly become slow and dull. Where has their energy gone?

I wonder if it is because today's business professionals have not identified daily goals, so when they arrive at work they are at a loss for what precisely to do. They cannot move briskly any more because they do not know what to do. This is a serious problem that may be negatively influencing the morale of an entire workplace without people realizing. We can certainly say that business professionals who proactively remember to move briskly are very competent at their work too. When there is even one business professional who is full of energy, the rest of the workers in the business could follow his/her example, however in reality this may be difficult. Some business people may just watch it in a detached, cold, and unemotional manner. In such a case, I suggest that supervisors take the lead. As I stated previously, it is important to say aloud, "Let's try our best today!" However, the more important thing is to reflect your excitement honestly in your movements.

THINK BEYOND YOUR BOSS

You are not truly an independent and capable business person if you wait to be ordered around. If you wait to be told what you must do you will never reach your full potential.

In order to become a person with greater capabilities and who has the ability to progress to a higher position you must work as if you are competing with your boss. This does not mean you need to go against him, but there is no need to be fearful of this way of working. Go beyond what your boss would normally tell you to do. It is necessary to anticipate and think ahead of the step you are currently at. This method of thinking, of respectful competition with your boss, will enable you to develop your work methods and challenge yourself.

I myself am the type of person to work at my own pace. "It looks like you are always spending your time leisurely. Why don't you work more seriously?" my boss when I worked at the Gifu Prefecture Productivity Center used to ask, implying that my work pace was slow. But this didn't bother me because the pace I was working at was more efficient than anyone else I worked with. I was confident that I could do my job better than my boss and increase sales more than anyone else. You should not be afraid to do your work, or of people questioning your work, if you are challenging yourself and exceeding everyone's expectations.

The important thing here is whether or not you can anticipate what work should be performed next. It is not that difficult. You can predict most of the time what instructions your boss is going to give you, once you understand his/her character well. More often than not your boss's orders are often overwhelmingly the same and consist of only about 400 words. The specific details may change but the content of the orders will be the same, more or less. It is important for people to understand this point, because understanding this means that anyone can stay one step ahead of their boss and easily increase their productivity.

It is also important to understand how we do this because the repetition of orders is a waste in itself. Most supervisors and managers do not notice that they are creating waste. Therefore it is important for employees to notice this, so that they can help eliminate the waste their bosses are creating. Your efforts of waste elimination will certainly be recognized.

It is said that the qualification of the first-class baseball player is his ability to accurately read how a pitcher throws a ball. The same thing applies to business people. You can become a first-class business professional when you anticipate the direction and work ahead of your boss's orders.

Yamada's Lean Lesson No. 30

"A student actively seeks teachers and initiates learning.
Subordinates only do what they are told to do.
Everyone must be a student!"

Photo 7: Yamada Training Session

5

常識を打ち破れ

Breaking the Mold

Change Your Attitude: Quit Waiting for Instructions

At my company, PEC, we hold report-out sessions with our trainees regarding Kaizen improvements within their respective companies. We hold these because I wholeheartedly believe that less and less people willingly think on their own and proactively put ideas into action. Why is that? I think it is because they are accustomed, beginning from childhood, to waiting for someone to tell them what to do. Parents buy things for their children even before the child asks for them in the hopes that their children will lack nothing. Children then grow up, go to school, then are told to go out and get jobs. Once they start working, monotonous and unimaginative employee training is waiting for them.

The training that begins at the earliest stage of education is nearly the exact same as what a person encounters at each company: standardized training materials and textbooks. In other words, people receive education and training entirely based on manuals.

This is no different from the Mass Production System by means of conveyor belt. Everyone is placed on a "conveyor belt" to become a uniform employee, whether they like it or not. They are like lions at a zoo that have lost their wild combative spirit. An animal handler feeds the lions, whether or not the lions are hungry. When this pattern becomes habit, the lions come to believe that their food is always given to them by their handler and as a result the lions lose their hunting instinct. If you are raised in a training environment where you are given orders before you are able to express your desire to do something, you become a person who cannot make a decision yourself.

Wherever society cannot be held responsible, and won't hold themselves responsible, for such a person, we face a crisis. We are currently living in an era where companies will sacrifice workers for their own survival, instead of focusing on investing in their employees. Given this, we must change our attitude of waiting to be instructed — be proactive instead of passive.

It was a long time ago when the saying, "Good things come to those who wait" was still valid. Today, you will get no lucky break if you wait for things to change.

APPLY MUDA-TORI TO REFLECT ON YOUR FAILURES

There are too many young people today who completely forget to reflect on their own failures. Instead of seeing a failure as a learning opportunity they lay blame for their own failures on society, their companies, bosses, and other people. Just to see how they react, ask a young business professional who made a mistake, "Why did you make such a mistake?" Most of them are likely to answer, "I only did what my boss told me to do." They lay the blame on their bosses without thinking because they have a notion that work related instructions always come from the top, from senior employees or management, and they believe they are supposed to just follow what their bosses tell them to do. There is nothing to gain from your mistakes if you only lay blame upon someone else.

Nothing positive will come out of your mistakes if you repeat the same mistakes over and over. It is said that "failure is the mother of success," however your failure will never become your success unless you reflect on your mistakes and attempt to find the true causes so you do not repeat the same mistakes over and over again. We should reflect upon our mistakes to eliminate the repetition of similar mistakes and stop laying blame on others. To start with, try to accept responsibility for your mistakes yourself. I am sure that you will begin to see a new direction from there.

Yamada's Lean Lesson No. 31

"Everyone wants to get paid for the least amount of work. Easy work can never lead to profitability.

If you simply do easy work each day, your company will not survive.

If you produce results that no one else can—then your company will become truly profitable."

DEVELOP YOUR ABILITY TO REACT TO CHANGING ENVIRONMENTS

It is a good idea to let children experience the real world so that they can grow into respectable adults. The same thing can be said about business professionals. If business professionals only associate with people in limited areas they can only develop limited capabilities. When your association is restricted to only colleagues in your department you may not be able to associate well with people in other departments.

One example that explains this point more directly is the poor association of people between different industries. Often when meeting people in a different industry, the conversation is similar to the following:

"What business are you in?"

"I am in the business of …"

"Is that right?"

Most of their conversations end like this. They do not attempt to ask any further questions because they are afraid of not understanding the other person's business. This may lead to serious consequences in both networking and your personal life if your understanding is very narrow and limited. You may even be at a complete loss when you are assigned to another department if you cannot relate and learn from this new group of people.

No matter where you go, what company you work for, flexibility and ready-to-use skills are required. It may be true that you feel at ease as long as you stay within your comfort zone, however, you may be digging your own grave that way. Do not think that you know enough already; instead, try to be conscious all the time about breaking out of your comfort zone and expanding your knowledge. If you become alert to the outside world you can strengthen your own abilities using the information you obtain. If you want to devote your life to becoming a business professional you need to make a great effort to break out of your own framework and broaden your association with people.

LEARNING FROM MISTAKES IS MORE IMPORTANT THAN PHILOSOPHICAL KNOWLEDGE

Would it be surprising to you if I were to say that classroom and book knowledge is largely unnecessary for business professionals? I believe we need training more than simply education. It is true that a person must understand the concepts of their business, but most of the job skills that are necessary beyond that understanding can and should be trained.

Business professionals basically do the same thing every day. However, they must constantly strive to deepen their skills and make their work more efficient, even if the content of their work is the same. Something must be improved every day in order to eliminate more waste. If you are a marketing person, your sales method should be improving each day. If you are an administrator, your work method should be changing for the better each day. If you are a receptionist, you want to improve your manner of dealing with customers each day.

How do we go about changing ourselves then? We make changes through training and trial & error, not through knowledge or education.

A true carpenter relies on a plane and his/her skills alone to determine the quality of his/her work. Improvement of his/her skills is key to achieving a greater result. There are no other ways to produce a better result except practicing day after day.

I am not saying that knowledge and education are unnecessary, however you do not need them in excess at the cost of actual hands-on learning and your precious time. What is needed is to improve your skills through training. Business professionals are basically the same as craftsmen, even if business people today do not understand, as in the carpenter example, what their plane and skills are. They are simply cutting trees and shaving wood blindly. They attempt to try a few ways of working and end up with unsatisfactory results. That blind method is nothing but waste. Business professionals need to know what the equivalent of their plane and skills are and devote themselves to training in order to improve the skills of their trade. People who continue their training can grow both personally and professionally.

Yamada's Lean Lesson No. 32

"Companies have stressed standardization too much and people have become standardized as a result. A person who can say "I'll leave such an over-standardized company" is a very important person.

A person who can do well without his/her job title is the real contributor of his/her company."

TRANSFORM KNOWLEDGE TO WISDOM THROUGH EXPERIENCE

Knowledge x Experience = Wisdom

This is my equation, which I believe to be correct based upon my experiences. No matter how much knowledge you may have, it does not become wisdom without experience. For example, suppose you understand how to peel an apple with a knife; it is still only knowledge. You can actually peel an apple skillfully with a knife by doing it. If you cut your finger while peeling the apple, you gain an understanding of how to handle a knife more safely, based on the experience you had. The wisdom that you acquire through your experience is vital to growing and learning.

People such as Mr. Soichiro Honda, who is the founder of Honda, have climbed to the top of their industry because of more than simply their knowledge. Their mistakes helped them accumulate their living wisdom, and their earlier mistakes helped shape their success. The wisdom they acquired through their experiences supported them and helped them move forward.

No matter how many business manuals you read, it is still only knowledge. Only when you actually put your knowledge into action will you understand the difference between what you learn and reality. It is a waste if you are afraid of putting your knowledge into action, no matter how diligently you cram knowledge into your head. The experiences that you accumulate are necessary in order to make the most of your knowledge.

Today, anyone can easily obtain a wide range of information and people tend to place less and less importance on their actual experiences. Your true capabilities, however, are determined by the depth of wisdom that you acquire from experience, not of how much knowledge you have. Virtual reality is becoming more common nowadays to try and replace what people learn based in real life, and that is why we need to take a step back and take another look at the power of wisdom through actual experience.

SHOW HOW TO IMPROVE ON THE GEMBA

Management believes that giving numerical values to target productivity is specific and useful. To a shop floor worker, however, this is useless information unless the steps to take in order to meet the target are also given.

We often hear conversations on the shop floor regarding targets that flow like this:

> "Let's target a 30% increase of production this morning."

> "Alright, we'll target at 30%."

Management sets a concrete number as their target and the entire company tries to reach the target. However, often they will not reach their target. Why is this?

As in the example above, most managers think they show their target clearly in real numbers, however, their instruction are not a clear and concrete set of instructions for workers on the production floor. Showing numbers in such a way is merely a calculation, not anything tangible to help workers achieve the often arbitrary feeling goal. Instead, you must give your instruction to increase productivity by 30% as follows:

"How much time does it take you to do this task now?"

"I think it takes about 10 seconds."

"Let's try to do it in 7 then."

"7 seconds?"

"If we can do it in 7 seconds, we can increase productivity by 30%."

A specific dialog and set of instructions shows workers a concrete action to take, thereby making your target clear. My instruction method is to teach management how to meet their goals by giving concrete instructions. I show them how to encourage workers to try to shorten 10 seconds to 9 seconds, 9 seconds to 8 seconds, and 8 seconds to 7 seconds. Motivation and livelihood across the workplace are born through their efforts.

Numbers in slogans certainly have some magical power that moves people, however it is far more effective to give instructions by showing actual actions that can be taken if you want to motivate people toward a goal. Show it in actions. Show it in pictures. Write and read your instructions. Speak your instructions. Make your instructions in this manner and you will succeed in achieving your goal. Allow and encourage people to take action instead of fretting over numbers in their head.

> ### *Yamada's Lean Lesson No. 33*
>
> "Management systems should not be solely based on principles—it is about achieving results by executing changes and ideas.
>
> Operations are not philosophy.
> Operations are to take action.
> No result will ever come out of doing nothing.
> Execute your actions instead of thinking about them."

BE CAUTIOUS WHEN BUSINESS GROWTH REACHES OVER 15%

Among the popular fables most people recognize is a story called "The Tortoise and the Hare." There are various interpretations of the moral of the story, but the most often recited interpretation is this: you do not need to be as speedy as the hare to win a race, you can win a race through perseverance, even if you are slow like the tortoise.

"Slow and Steady Wins the Race"

As one example, let's think about facility equipment. If what you are looking for is fast production speed, the investment capital necessary for production equipment increases exponentially. To simplify the matter, suppose one machine that can produce 100 products costs $10,000, you will need equipment that costs $40,000 to produce 200 products. Sooner or later this will lead to excessive production as companies attempt to justify the cost of the machine by producing more products they hope to sell.

A typical example is the steel industry. Steel companies increase their production volume by aggressive investments in new equipment, but the outcome is often unsuccessful due to large inventory caused by low demand. It is dangerous to attempt to increase production too fast because it may drastically imbalance production and demand. In the IT industry, many companies once saw a drastic increase of their sales; often by as much as 50% or 60% compared with the previous year. They continued their capital investment believing the growth would continue even further. However, their businesses did not grow as expected and they began to steadily lose money.

In the manufacturing industry, a growth of 10% is considered to be very good but we must be cautious if the growth reaches around 15%. A 15% increase indicates to other companies that there is space for competition. In addition, more new companies merge in high growth business environments leading to tougher business competition. Worse yet, there may be a danger that these companies will go under together.

Your health, for example, loses its balance when your height or weight increase suddenly. Along the same vein, it is desirable to maintain well balanced, moderate business growth rather than sudden leaps of growth.

OPPORTUNITIES ARE HIDDEN IN PROBLEMS

In the Toyota Production System workers are told to "Stop the production line when there is a problem." However, people often don't understand the true meaning because this idea goes against the common knowledge of manufacturing—remove the defective piece and fix the issue at a later time. This may seem rational but is actually the biggest and most costly mistake a company can make.

When we say "stop the production line," it means to stop the line IMMEDIATELY at THE LOCATION a problem occurs at. Mr. Ohno did not mean to stop a production line at a later time. It makes it easier to find a solution if you respond to a problem immediately.

Solving a problem at the production line can be understood by the analogy of a police officer arresting a criminal at the scene of the crime. They don't see a crime happening and let the criminal get away, thinking they can catch him at a later date. It is important to act immediately at the location where the problem occurred. The reality on real manufacturing floors, however, is that people make excuses saying, "We must achieve the production volume" or "We must meet the shipping schedule" and tend to delay solving problems. As a result, the problem remains unsolved and the same thing is repeated every day. This is a reproduction of waste.

We see similar examples in business people's work environments. They are expected to respond to a problem immediately, however, it is imperative to dig for the real cause of the problem instead of just looking at the issue on the surface. Problem solving should be a root cause treatment and not simply a treatment of the symptoms. It is the same thing as taking aspirin when you have a fever; it does not solve everything it simply reduces the symptoms. The fever may be caused by some serious internal ailment. It is important to dig deeper to find a root cause by asking yourself "what caused the fever?" instead of thinking "lower the fever."

It is said that business opportunities are hidden in problems. That means we begin to see a new business direction only through serious problem solving efforts and by relentlessly seeking root causes. It is necessary to brace yourself and challenge problems instead of delaying or running away from problems. Work is a continuous effort of solving problems and a person's work style is clearly shown by looking at how he/she responds to problems.

From a different perspective, a workplace is a reservoir of problems. Muda, Mura, and Muri (Waste, Variability, Overworking) are generated as if they are supposed to happen, thus one problem creates a new problem, one after another. We need to reflect upon how we work to find out if we are just letting each day pass by without making an effort to find the root causes of problems.

> ### *Yamada's Lean Lesson No. 34*
>
> "Kaizen, the point of overcoming common knowledge, is the base for everything.
> Kaizen is endless and limitless.
> If you can find one minute of Muda you will nurture your eyes to see Muda and soon you will be able to find one second of Muda.
> Question yourself about every motion."

HAVE THE COURAGE TO QUESTION "HOW IT'S ALWAYS BEEN DONE"

Mr. Sakichi Toyoda, the forefather of Toyota Automobiles, is known for his development of the automatic weaver, which came about through many years of tireless research on manual weaving looms. What triggered his research was the manual weaving loom on which his mother worked very hard.

"I want to make her work easier," he later explained. He observed how she worked with her weaving loom and asked himself why this motion was necessary. It was Mr. Ohno who said, "Kaizen on the manufacturing floors starts from asking yourself why you are doing this now." Asking "Why?" is the key to solving a problem.

Something in common between these two people is asking the question "Why?". Mr. Toyoda's research to answer the question that came to his mind when he watched his mother work led to the subsequent development of automatic weaving looms, and further on to the establishment of the Toyota Production System. When you are doing the same work every day in the same process, you believe that the way you are doing your work is the best way to work and it doesn't dawn upon you to ask yourself why you are doing your work the way you are. Without stopping to ask yourself why instead of taking the process for granted no progress can be made.

Mr. Ohno says to repeat "Why?" five times. For example:

WHY did the machine stop?

> Because the fuse is blown out due to overloading.

WHY is it overloading?

> Because the lubrication of the lower bearing is insufficient.

WHY didn't it lubricate sufficiently?

> Because the lubrication pump is not pumping lubricant sufficiently.

WHY is the pump not pumping well?

> Because the shaft of the pump is worn out.

WHY did it wear out?

> Because there is no filter and some metal powder gets mixed in with the lubricant.

Thus by repeating "Why?" five times, you will naturally find the solution to solving your problem and applying Kaizen. We should be mindful about stopping for a moment each day and asking yourself "Why?" in order to overcome your habits every day. Once you make it a habit to stop your hands and feet and ask yourself why you are doing something the way you are, you can change your attitude and enthusiasm toward work.

DISPROVE "COMMON SENSE" WITH BREAKTHROUGH IDEAS

The Japanese seem like a people who cherish "common sense" ideas as if they are the golden rules. People accept their common knowledge of how business and life should work reverently without any doubt. However, people cannot overcome their current situation as long as they continue to simply operate under their understanding of common knowledge. You find joy in your work only when you continue your effort to overcome your current situation and steadily improve your abilities each day. In this regard, the first thing we need to do is to discover ideas that will help us overcome our common knowledge.

When you are challenging what people consider common knowledge, or common sense, you will often come across resistance. During a factory reform, 99% of people may be against the new way you are proposing simply because you are attempting to change their common knowledge of how business is run. Most people generally do not like change, which I feel is the biggest trouble factor in a factory reform. In other words, attempting factory improvement generally means to venture into doing things that 99 out of 100 people oppose.

In order to overcome resistance you must stand by your changes and show people that the new methods achieve more advantageous results. Once the transformation is moving in a desirable direction, you will receive more understanding responses from more people. Once people understand Kaikaku, or radical change for the better, more people will respond to your call for change, and the reform will eventually become your new common knowledge of how the business runs. Once this happens you can begin the cycle once more, questioning how you are working and creating a new and better way of working.

Common knowledge is not something we should keep faithfully forever but should be something that transforms itself to become a new one, fostering Kaizen and continuously improving. Both Muda-tori and the Toyota Production System were born from the point where the new ideas overcame the old common knowledge. Today, the Internet is widely spread and people share all sorts of information. Because of this it is easy to seek different ways of thinking and looking at problems, sparking people's creativity and creating a platform for reform unlike any we have witnessed in the past.

Are we going to be buried under the old common

knowledge or are we going to overcome the old common knowledge to become more competitive? We are now faced with the choice between the two.

> ### *Yamada's Lean Lesson No. 35*
> *"Act with clear objectives and think about how you can be #1 in your industry. To work is to win against the competition— that provides you with a sense of reward and fulfillment."*

WORK SHOULD FULFILL AND CHALLENGE YOU

Work is something that you must do to truly live. There is a saying, "Work is the spice that adds flavor to your life." Work is an indispensable element to live a life that has flavor. Unfortunately, through the development of capitalism and the industrial revolution, people are most often forced to work like slaves. People now work in order to simply make a living, regardless of whether or not they like or enjoy their work. Before we truly realized it, work became the means to make a living rather than the seasoning to make our lives flavorful.

What has happened as a result? We have lost our pride in our work. The only thing left that you may be proud of is that you could find a job at a large or famous company. Now, though, even the company a person works for is no longer a source of pride because in the world we live in today the continued existence of a company is uncertain at best. In this environment many people adopt a clear cut attitude, separating their personal life from their work and only seek enjoyment and a sense of fulfillment outside of their work. In my view, however, no matter what kind of work you do, you can find a sense of fulfillment in work because work is there for you all the time. Volunteer work, for example, can be your enjoyment because you have work to do when volunteering.

Our lives are not truly fulfilled without fulfilling work.

Work Is One of Our Self-Expressions

Many people believe that work means to withstand pains in order to make money. I think this is a very wrong idea. I believe that work is one of our self-expressions. There is a book that I read when I was in my 20s that moved me very much titled "Sony Motivates People."

In the book there is a woman whose job is to clean the bathrooms. Sony, in those days, had a problem with graffiti in the bathrooms. The cleaning lady erased the graffiti diligently, but no matter how hard she worked soon someone would scribble graffiti in the bathrooms again. For the cleaning lady, the bathrooms were her workplace and cleaning is important work, with the bathroom's cleanliness a source of pride. Thus she could not tolerate graffiti in her workplace. One day she posted a sign in the bathroom which said, "This is my workplace. Do not write graffiti." Suddenly the graffiti stopped. Everyone there understood her pride in her work and respected her more for standing up for her workplace.

There may be some people who think that her job was only cleaning toilets. However, for someone whose work is cleaning bathrooms, bathrooms are her/his workplace. Just like a business professional's workplace, bathrooms are simply the location of their self-expression. That is the reason why the woman could not tolerate graffiti.

Work should be like this for everyone, shouldn't it? Out of 24 hours a day, we spend typically 8 hours at work, and at least 1/3 of this time becomes waste unless we tackle our work as our self-expression. If we think of work as the ultimate stage on which we can express ourselves, we will want to do our work a little better each day and to greater satisfaction. There is no way to spend 1/3 of a day without expressing ourselves, even if we focus on work only being work and not a place to find enjoyment. However, if we can find pleasures in our work we can continue our work for a very long time. People gain wisdom through their work and can become true people through their work.

Work is our self-expression. With that awareness, we become enthusiastic to transform our work for the better each day.

Afterword

Mass production and mass selling, which originated in the U.S., has taken a firm hold on people around the world, where everyone now desires buying good products at a cheap price. The astonishing industrial waves in China, with its 1.2 billion population, has been threatening even the manufacturers in the advanced nations.

Competition between companies who sell products in large volumes is becoming fierce. Today, industrial products are expected to cost little to nothing, making it very difficult to maintain constant product prices. Each year companies are forced to reduce manufacturing costs, and company restructuring and factory closures are becoming common place. Those who choose to manufacturer through the use of mass production can no longer survive.

Even with this knowledge, standardization continues to progress and the work environment is filled with all kinds of regulations, from standard processes on manufacturing floors, to processes based on manuals, to obtaining ISO certification. All this standardization makes it very difficult for workers to accomplish anything through the motivation to improve alone. Even education is becoming more standardized and the wages of college graduates have become almost uniform across Japan, regardless what students study at school. It almost seems like this standardization has deprived students of their will to study.

The Toyota Production System that I have continued to experiment with aims at finding the huge wastes that are hidden in mass production and mass sales to eliminate the symbol of the Mass Production System, the conveyor belt. Each person can experience the effects of the Cell Production System and Single Stall System through Muda-tori to rebuild the manufacturing industry. People on the manufacturing floors at Sony and Canon have acquired Muda-tori techniques and continued their Kaizen effort to hugely affect the profitability of their company. Today, there are many people around me who have found fulfillment in their lives by finding and eliminating waste and applying their innovative ideas to their work. Muda-tori techniques help people find joy in their work and provide a faster way to reach their goals in life.

The 35 Yamada's Lean Lessons in this book are the collections of my voice at various occasions, compiled by fellow workers on the manufacturing floors I have visited. I hope that you will keep many of the sayings in your mind.

Hitoshi Yamada

Yamada's Lean Lessons

Yamada's Lean Lesson No. 8   39

"The focus today should be on quality of labor, not quality of products. If labor quality is improved, product quality will be assured.

You only deserve more than an average salary if you do something above average—perform with better quality to achieve and receive more."

Yamada's Lean Lesson No. 9   44

"You are a true manufacturer if you can produce a high variety of more expensive products with as little workspace, as few workers, and least expensive equipment as possible.

If you do that you will win customer satisfaction, whose quality of life you have increased. If you can achieve that, each worker becomes more important and their skills become invaluable.."

Yamada's Lean Lesson No. 10   50

"Muda-tori is possible if you try to finish 8 hours' worth of tasks in 4 hours a day. You need to understand how the work needs to be completed in order to complete tasks in half the time—you must standardize the process."

YAMADA'S LEAN LESSON NO. 15   71

"The Principle of Manufacturing "Don't
produce items that don't sell" has been
overshadowed by the idea of abundance.
One thing that is overly abundant is information, which results in forecasting based
on something other than true needs.
This concept is embodied within agriculture as "Hosaku Binbo", meaning the
impoverishment of farmers despite a bum-
per harvest."

YAMADA'S LEAN LESSON NO. 16   75

"Creating an organizational culture that
is able to change and adapt is more important that having an abundance of
resources.
An organization's strength is built upon
this adaptable culture."

YAMADA'S LEAN LESSON NO. 17   78

"Companies often evaluate their organization by profitability not by the commitment of employees. Changes in profitability will only change if the organizational
mindset changes. True results can only be
achieved by changing individual mindset."

YAMADA'S LEAN LESSON No. 18 84

"Solid production management is as important as the contractor's plans for building a house. Operations must be adjusted accordingly for everything to be completed together, and in the proper order.
If there is no skill in the operations, we call it "Sechin Daiku" (an unskilled carpenter)."

YAMADA'S LEAN LESSON No. 19 87

"Manufacturers must regain the ability to read a factory. If you lose this ability to read a plant, you will not get a second chance to stand on your own two feet again.
Without the ability to read a factory, the opportunity to recover is lost forever."

YAMADA'S LEAN LESSON No. 20 92

"People who do not question how they perform their work can never eliminate Muda.
The starting point for identifying and eliminating waste is to question how work is performed."

YAMADA'S LEAN LESSON No. 21 96

"Develop a strong desire to carry out what you have learned.
It is more important to apply your knowledge to your work than to simply learn."

then review, adjust, and perform the task. Try it right away & review it—Don't simply plan and think about it."

Yamada's Lean Lesson No. 29

"Unless you change your mindset, your actions will not change.
Work quickly with an energetic voice to change your mindset. This is the starting point to changing your actions."

Yamada's Lean Lesson No. 30

130

"A student actively seeks teachers and initiates learning.
Subordinates only do what they are told to do.
Everyone must be a student!"

Yamada's Lean Lesson No. 31

134

"Everyone wants to get paid for the least amount of work. Easy work can never lead to profitability.
If you simply do easy work each day, your company will not survive.
If you produce results that no one else can—then your company will become truly profitable."

"Companies have stressed standardization too much and people have become standardized as a result. A person who can say "I'll leave such an over-standardized company" is a very important person.
A person who can do well without his/her job title is the real contributor of his/her company."

"Management systems should not be solely based on principles—it is about achieving results by executing changes and ideas.
Operations are not philosophy.
Operations are to take action.
No result will ever come out of doing nothing.
Execute your actions instead of thinking about them."

"Kaizen, the point of overcoming common knowledge, is the base for everything.
Kaizen is endless and limitless.
If you can find one minute of Muda you will nurture your eyes to see Muda and soon you will be able to find one second of Muda.
Question yourself about every motion."

"Act with clear objectives and think about
how you can be #1 in your industry. To
work is to win against the competition—
that provides you with a sense of reward
and fulfillment."

Index

I

J

K

P

R

S

W

Y

Publications from Enna

From Enna's new classics by Shigeo Shingo to our Lean Origin Series, Enna provides companies with the foundation of knowledge and practical implementation ideas that will ensure your efforts to internalize process improvement. Reach your vision and mission with the expertise within these world-class texts. Call toll-free (866) 249-7348 or visit us on the web at www.enna.com to order or request our free product catalog.

100% Leadership

There is no recipe for success. If there were, we would all use it and it would cease to be effective. Yet, there are many roads that can lead to success. The secret is to choose the right road for your organization among all options. For leaders at all levels, this book provides guidelines for daily decisions and actions, as well as guidance on communication, team-building, planning, and efficiency.

ISBN 978-1-897363-98-0 | 2008 | $21.99 | Item: **915**

Kaizen and the Art of Creative Thinking

Read the book that New York Times Best Selling author of *The Toyota Way*, Jeffrey Liker says, "will help you understand the deep thinking that underlies the real practice of TPS." Dr. Shigeo Shingo's Scientific Thinking Mechanism is the framework from which Toyota and hundreds of other companies have utilized to manage creative problem solving.

ISBN 978-1-897363-59-1 | 2007 | $59.40 | Item: **909**

Twelve Keys to Sustainable Company Success

A must have for companies of any size looking to achieve and sustain long-terms success. Christopher & Thor condense their extensive years of business knowledge and experience into an easy to follow guide of important points, or keys, that all organizations should take into consideration when it comes to running their business. These keys are for *all* fields of work in any industry.

ISBN 978-1-926537-22-1 | 2011 | $19.95 | Item: **931**

Fundamental Principles

Fundamental Principles of Lean Manufacturing is the latest discovered and newly translated classic from Dr. Shigeo Shingo, engineering genius and a driving force behind the successful realization of the Toyota Production System and Lean Manufacturing. This first-time-in-translation book gives modern readers total access to the fundamentals of improving any  process. Again, Dr. Shingo amazes and provides you with even more tools to take advantage of in order to solve your problems and pursue a course toward improvement.

ISBN 978-1-897363-07-8 | 2009 | $64.80 | Item: **921**

Mistaken Kanbans

Let Mistaken Kanbans be your roadmap to guide you through the steps necessary to implement and successful Kanban System. This book will help you to not only understand the complexities of a Kanban System but gives you the tools necessary, and the guidance through real-life lessons learned, to avoid disastrous consequences related to the improper use of such systems.

ISBN 978-1-926537-10-8 | 2009 | $27.99 | Item: **919**

Toyota Mindset

From the brilliant mind of a legend in the LEAN manufacturing world comes the reasoning behind the importance of using your intellect, challenging your workers and why continuous improvement is so important. For anyone who wishes to gain insight into how the Toyota Production System came to be or wants to know more about the person behind TPS this book is a must read!

ISBN 978-1-926537-11-5 | 2009 | $34.99 | Item: **920**

Clinical 5S

It is no secret that problem areas are abundant within the healthcare industry, but what if you could reduce or even eliminate these problems? By utilizing the Lean tools that Mr. Takahara has cultivated and perfected in the healthcare industry, you will be able to do just that. Clinical 5S walks you through how to create a better functioning, less problematic workplace and provides you with the tools and methodology for success.

ISBN 978-1-926537-19-1 | 2011 | $45.99 | Item: **930**

Toyota Way in Sales and Marketing

Many companies today are trying to implement the ideas and principles of Lean into non-traditional environments, such as service centers, sales organizations and transactional environments. In this book Mr. Ishizaka provides insight on how to apply Lean operational principles and Kaizen to these dynamic and complicated environments.

ISBN 978-1-926537-08-5 | 2009 | $28.99 | Item: **918**

Study Mission to Japan

We are excited to present an exclusive trip to the birthplace of Lean. We provide a one-week unique tour at a reasonable all-inclusive price that will guide you to a better understanding of Lean Manufacturing principles. Enna has exclusive access to Toyota and Toyota suppliers due to our publications of Dr. Shigeo Shingo's classic manuscripts. You will have one-on-one access to Japanese Lean Executives and learn from their experiences and solutions. We also offer custom private tours for executive management teams over 12 people. Join us on our next tour by visiting www.enna.com/japantrip and register on-line or by telephone at: +1 (360) 306-5369.

To Order:

Mail orders and checks to:
Enna Products Corporation
ATTN: Order Processing
1602 Carolina Street, Unit B3
Bellingham, WA 98229, USA
Phone: +1 (360) 306-5369 • Fax: (905) 481-0756
Email: info@enna.com

We accept checks and all major credit cards.

Notice: All prices are in US Dollars and are subject to change without notice.

For Product Safety Concerns and Information please contact our EU representative GPSR@taylorandfrancis.com Taylor & Francis Verlag GmbH, Kaufingerstraße 24, 80331 München, Germany

Printed and bound by CPI Group (UK) Ltd, Croydon, CR0 4YY
08/06/2025
01897003-0002